# GUIDE TO CONTENTMENT

# Guide
## to
# Contentment

FULTON J. SHEEN

ST PAULS

Library of Congress Cataloging-in-Publication Data

Sheen, Fulton J. (Fulton John), 1895-1979.
    Guide to contentment / Fulton J. Sheen.
        p.    cm.
    Rev. ed. of: Fulton J. Sheen's guide to contentment.   1967.
    ISBN 0-8189-0773-8
    1. Christian life — Catholic authors.   2. Peace of mind —
Religious aspects — Catholic Church. 3. Contentment —    Religious aspects — Christianity. 4. Catholic Church —    Doctrines.   I.
Sheen, Fulton J. (Fulton John), 1895-1979.    Fulton J. Sheen's
guide to contentment.    II. Title.
    BX2350.2.S44      1996
    248.4'82 — dc20                                        96-29429
                                                              CIP

This Alba House edition is published by special arrangement
with the Estate of Fulton J. Sheen and the Society for the
Propagation of the Faith, 366 Fifth Avenue, New York, NY 10001.

This book is published in the United States of America
by Alba House, the publishing arm of the Society of St. Paul,
an international religious congregation of priests and brothers
serving the Church through the communications media.

ISBN: 0-8189-0773-8

**Printing Information:**

Current Printing - first digit           5  6  7  8  9  10

Year of Current Printing - first year shown

                                       2010   2011   2012

# Table of Contents

## Our Needs and Their Fulfillment

## The Nature of Our Minds

## Our Searchings

## Table of Contents

### THE WAY TO ACCEPTANCE

### NEIGHBORLINESS

### DOCTRINES AND NATIONS

## ABIDING IN PEACE

# HOW WE ARE TORN

## Compulsion I

"I am a compulsive drinker." "She is a compulsive eater." "I don't know what made me do it; I just heard a voice." These are the excuses one hears daily, implying that the will is no longer free, but as if under the direction of another.

Is there such a thing as compulsion? Definitely. How does it come about? Generally through three stages: consent, act and habit. Every person has buried in his subconsciousness certain powers, capacities or impulses given for his perfection. One refers to our body, the other to our mind, and the last to things outside the body and mind. The first is sex or the creative impulse; the other is a desire for power, e.g., through a search for truth or the pursuit of a talent or the right use of power. But outside of the body and the mind, there are things. The person is finally driven to possess property. Just as the will is free because a man can call his soul his own, so property is external and an economic guarantee of human freedom.

Each of these impulses is capable of being perverted. Fire on the hearth is good, but fire in the clothes closet is not. The sex instinct can be distorted into license and perversion. In that case, the other person is really not loved, but is used. One drinks the water; one forgets the glass. Hidden in our nature is a lot of flammable material which is not ignited except by some suggestion from without, with the consent of the will. External influences only tempt; they do not compel. There is no inseparable connection between the two. When Joseph was tempted by Potiphar's wife he said, "How could I commit so great a wrong and thus stand condemned before God?"

The mind's desire for knowledge and truth can be perverted by each person saying to himself, "There will be no measure of truth or knowledge outside of *me*. Whatever *I* decide to be true is true. *I* make the truth. *I* make the law. *I* am my own creator. *I* am my own savior." The drive for the possession of things can be turned into avarice, greed, selfishness and the refusal to help the poor.

When does the good impulse become tempted? It becomes tempted generally by a solicitation from without. For example, the sex impulse might be perverted by a picture, a book, a person. There is no perversion at this particular point; there is only a suggestion. This is what is called temptation to do something immoral. No temptation to do evil is wrong in itself; it is only the consent which is wrong.

It has been said that it is wrong to repress our impulses. No! Repression is not always wrong. As a matter of fact, every expression of something good, e.g., to give food to a hungry person, is a repression of selfishness.

When an outside evil pleasure is presented, our nature exaggerates the proportions of everything; it shows the pleasure or the profit through a magnifying glass, multiplied by desire and expectation. One can imagine a mountain of gold, but one can never see a mountain of gold. What the imagination does is to present things to the mind *not as they are*, but as the mind *would have them to be*. Notice that all love songs are songs of expectation. Nothing cheats a man as much as expectation, which promises a lot but delivers nothing.

The desire to pervert our good impulses means that the subjective and the objective meet; that which before was only within the heart now begins to feel the touch and the allure of something outside. As Shakespeare said:

> How oft the sight of means to do ill deeds
> Make deeds ill done!

After the consent of the will to do what is wrong, comes the deed. As the boy grows into a man, so the will grows into the act.

Once the wrong act is done, there follows the uneasiness and remorse which is actually God calling the soul back to itself. The act repeated many times turns into habits. They are like tiny strands of silk, any one of which can be readily broken, but when woven day after day, they become a great chain which no giant can break. Habits tend to create or strengthen an attitude and disposition. They become so very natural that we are hardly conscious of them, whether good or bad. All the good things lie downstream, and all we have to do is just float like a log. When finally the habit creates a rut in our brain so that we automatically respond to any temptation, we have what is called "compulsion."

## Compulsion II

It has been stated that flammable material exists on the inside of every human being. For example, the righteous use of sex could be perverted into grossness; a desire for perfection could turn one into a tyrant; and the desire for property as the extension of oneself, into a miser. The stages by which one advances into compulsion are: first, the consent of the will to any temptation; next, the act which is the result of the temptation; and, finally, the habit itself. It takes many acts to make a habit, as it takes many strands of flax to make a rope.

Habits are good as well as bad. How weary our brain would be if we had to relearn playing the piano each time we sat down to it, or if we had to go through the laborious process of learning to write when we composed a letter. In the case of evil habits, such as alcoholism, the energy which once went into the will to prevent an excess now goes into the habit itself to enforce it. Conscience, which at first registered a protest against an evil action such as hurting a neighbor, becomes dulled from abuse. It is very much like the spring on a screen door during the summertime; it loses its resiliency and ability to close to keep out flies. Good acts make virtue easier, and evil acts make vice easier. The hedge broken down is easier to get through. The drops of water flowing through a dike can eventually end in a flood.

How habits eventually lead to compulsion may be illustrated by the parable of the trees of the forest who had a solemn parliament in which they decided to enact some laws against the wrongs which the ax had done them. They finally agreed that no tree would lend wood as a handle for an ax under the pain of being outlawed by the other trees. The ax without a handle traveled up and down the forest and begged for wood from cedar, ash, oak and elm, but no one would lend him a chip. At last he went to the briars near the trunks of the trees and said to the trees that these shrubs were sucking away the chemicals of the soil, and were also obscuring the glory of the fair trees. The trees agreed to give him a handle to cut down the shrubs, but when the ax got the handle, he cut the trees down also.

When a strong man has a palace that is well defended, he can keep his goods in peace. But when one stronger than he attacks the palace, then he loses his goods and also his liberty. In like manner, there eventually comes to some habitual practice of vice what is known as compulsion. Within the course of one evening, two young mothers in an Eastern city were assaulted by a man who broke down the front door, saying, "I am a compulsive sex maniac." There are five million alcoholics in the United States, most of whom would say, "I can't help it, I am a compulsive drinker. The sight of alcohol triggers me, and I have no power to resist."

It is at this point that psychiatrists and social workers and others say with some degree of justice that such people are sick. Indeed they are sick, but they are not sick in the same way as a person with cancer who never willed that the cancer should invade his body or that it should be multiplied within him as a kind of a habit. But all who suffer from a so-called compulsion have entered into this state as a result of successive repeated acts, until a point was reached where, as a great Russian writer has said, "unlimited freedom leads to unlimited tyranny."

What must be stressed is that no human will is ever completely ruined by a force on the outside. It can, like a muscle, be cut successively by a knife until the limb drops helpless. What is strange about the compulsion is that although the pleasure attached to the indulgence lessens with each successive indulgence, the power of compulsion increases. The energy that once went into the enjoyment now goes into forging new links in a chain which can be broken only with the greatest difficulty.

## Compulsion III

We have explained how successive acts can become habits, and how evil habits can eventually create compulsions in which one justifies himself, saying, "I cannot help it; I am a compulsive drinker," or "I am a compulsive sex maniac," or "I am a compulsive kleptomaniac." What emotions and feelings are associated with those under compulsion? First, almost all generally excuse themselves of any guilt. The blame is outside of them, not inside. This has been the story of human nature from the beginning when Adam blamed Eve and Eve blamed the serpent. It will generally be found that all who are given to some so-called compulsive vice will generally seek out the companionship of those who will never blame them, but rather excuse them; that is, a kind of a confraternity of "innocent babes" is formed by which they insulate themselves from any "moral corruption."

The second effect of the compulsion is the feeling of being divided and torn. It is as if one said, "My name is Legion." The person under compulsion feels very much like the hand when a burning coal is placed upon it; there is no true affinity between the nature of the hand and the nature of a burning coal. This attempt to merge or unite both creates pain. In like manner, it is not the nature of a body to be no longer master of its own fate and destiny. Something is in the mind which is alien to it. Like Macbeth, it asks:

> *Why do I yield to that suggestion*
> *Whose horrid image doth unfix my hair*
> *And make my seated heart knock at my ribs,*
> *Against the use of nature?*

The burning sensation inside of the human psyche means that there is something there which ought not to be there. There is going on inside the one under compulsion something of the struggle of two earthen pots swimming upon the water with the motto: "If we knock together, we sink together." There seems to be a knocking going on in the soul with the prospect of destruction.

A third note of compulsion, and one which closely follows the sensation of duality, is the realization that one cannot be under compulsion except through something other than the ego. That is why a compulsive drinker will say, "I am not to blame! I am under compulsion." No one has better described compulsion than Helmut Thielicke: "I belong to the demonic power, not simply in the sense of belonging to an alien master against my own will. Rather, I belong to that power in the sense that I belong to myself. That is to say, I cannot plead that it simply has control over me and that because of this coercion I incur no responsibility. No, this demonic bondage exists only as I belong to myself, to my ambition, to my self-assertiveness, my passions. The devil lives in the medium of my love of self. I do not love the devil by name, rather I love myself by name and precisely in doing this I deliver myself over to him. Even though I am here dealing with myself, it nevertheless becomes clear that in the very act of doing this, I am dealing with another, simply because I cannot break the bond in which I am held, and am, so to speak, forcibly bound to myself. I see a powerful spell hovering over this bondage."

Goethe's magician's apprentice said, "Those spirits I conjured up, now I can't get rid of them," which is a fairly good description of one under compulsion. But the case is not hopeless. Because there seems to be a power that is overwhelming one who is under compulsion, it follows that only another power is able to master it. In the last analysis, no love is ever driven out; it is only conquered by another love. One cannot overcome a love of alcohol until he finds some other love which is more compelling. One alcoholic told me that nothing and no person ever was able to convince him of the harm he was doing until he saw how it was ruining his wife. It was the love of the wife which eventually drove out the love of alcohol. The deepest mystery, therefore, appears in this final conflict of our human spirit with the Spirit of God, and it is only the power of the latter which can drive out and conquer the temporary holder of our human bondage.

# THE TIME OF YOUTH

## Polarization

Once boys and girls become teenagers, they tend to polarize or to separate into their own groups, boys with boys, girls with girls. The natural differentiation permits a true physical and psychic development of each. These negative and positive poles are necessary at a certain point in life, otherwise no sparks will be generated later. Where this polarization is not developed, due to a seriousness in love developed at a very early state, there is often an arrested development. The bow and violin are brought together before the bow is waxed and the strings are tuned. Young people are led into the big league before an apprenticeship in the minors. Young men and women do not want in others the qualities which they already possess, but the qualities which they do not. Everyone in love is looking for a complement, a difference, a filling up of what he or she lacks.

The next stage to polarization is what might be called divinization, in which the brain becomes clouded with erotic vapors which make one see divinity in humanity. Though there is a tendency at this stage to repudiate genuine religious worship, nevertheless, the language of religion is taken over in such words as "worship" and "eternity" and "loving forever." The Devil in Goethe says, "After drinking that draught you will see Helen of Troy in every woman."

The divinization has its basis in the fact that we have a soul as well as a body, and the soul, being infinite, can imagine infinite happiness. We can, for example, imagine a mountain of gold, but we will never see one. All experiences are colored with the brush of infinity, which accounts for this divinization in which the other partner becomes either a god or an angel.

Divinization is also a kind of crystallization. A piece of wood left for a time in the Salzburg salt mines will become covered with crystals which make it appear as if it were a mass of glittering jewels. This crystallization stage means that the young people do not actually fall in love with a person; they may fall in love with an *experience* because all is sweetness and light. There is a danger of projecting what one would like to find in another so that what is loved is not so much the other person as the projected image. "Falling in Love with Love" is the song side of this love of the impersonal instead of the personal. Sex is replaceable; a person is not.

## *The Experience of Love*

Many young people who think they're in love are actually falling in love with the experience of love. Because the other person gives a "glow," qualities are attributed to him or her which do not exist. She marries a "hero" and lives with a husband; he marries a "goddess" and lives with a wife.

Just suppose that while talking to you, I began tapping the pencil upon a table. You would notice it and perhaps consider that act strange. But if I did it every day, eventually you would not notice it. In order to bring it to your attention, I would have to pound much harder on the table each succeeding day. This is an indication of how sensations and feelings wear thin. If, therefore, a marriage is based wholly upon feeling and emotion, then love dies when the emotion dies. But where there is a love of the person because of the nobility of character and good-heartedness, then love never ends, but increases from day to day. An old German proverb states, "When love is young, it bubbles like new wine; the more it ages and grows clear, the more it becomes still."

A young man may know and appreciate a number of young women, and yet in the depths of his soul remain unmoved. And then one day, a woman with no conscious purpose will release some secret spring in the depths of his personality, and from that moment on, she becomes the center of his world.

What creates this new condition? It may have been knowledge of her character and personality, but it may also have been rather spontaneous, or what is called love at first sight.

One may ask if each of us does not really carry in his or her own heart a blueprint of the one that he or she loves. This blueprint is made by our reading, our prayers, our experiences, our hopes, our ideals, by our mother and father. Then suddenly, the ideal becomes concretized and realized in a person, and we say, "This is it!"

Each of us carries around in his own heart the music that he loves. We hear a certain kind of music for the first time, and we immediately love it. It satisfies the rhythm and the tempo that are already inside our hearts. Love at first sight may be incomprehensible, but it is a fact, nonetheless. In the end it may not be first sight; it may be just a dream coming true.

Beauty in a woman and strength in a man are two of the most evident spurs to love. Physical beauty and vitality increase vigor in each other, but it is to be noticed that beauty in a woman and strength in a man are given by God to serve purposes of allurement. They come at that age of life when men and women are urged to marry one another.

They are not permanent possessions. They are something like the frosting on a cake, or like the electric starter of an automobile motor. If love were based only on the fact that she is a model and he is a fullback on a football team, marriage would never endure. But just as the frosting on the cake leads to the cake itself, so too do these allurements pass on to greater treasures.

Once on congratulating a wife who had a very handsome husband, we heard her reply, "I no longer notice that he is handsome; I notice now that he has greater qualities."

## Our Love

Two great gifts are given to the young at a time when the family is meant to be founded, namely, beauty in a woman, and strength and power in a man. The least permanent of all gifts, they appear at a time when they were meant to serve purposes of allurement. Power is soon sapped, as athletes reach their point of retirement shortly after thirty. Beauty has two elements: one is surprise, and the other is love in the eyes of the beholder.

Because surprise is essential, the man who marries a beautiful woman may become so used to her beauty that he never sees it. Unless there is a deepening of the concept of beauty in the sense that he finds beauty of heart and soul and virtue within, mere physical loveliness is apt to fade. When love goes, beauty seems less beautiful.

Marriage is something like television; it eats up material and no one wants to see it again. Other men will tell the husband about the beauty of the wife, and women will tell the wife about the charm of the husband. Too infrequently it is noted that many husbands and wives are more amusing when they are not together. Wives sometimes cannot understand why others enjoy the company of their husbands, and vice versa. This is because each can tell the same old things to a new audience.

One is not to be a cynic about power and beauty. Though they are passing gifts of life, nevertheless they were meant to be renewed. Every boy that is born to the couple is a rebirth of power, and every daughter is a rebirth of beauty. Baby-talk becomes cute once again; new mysteries are unfolded, namely, fathercraft and mothercraft, as the husband and wife see themselves as sculptors quarrying new images from the block of humanity. The words of religion used in courtship such as "heaven" and "beautiful" now appear to have a new meaning; for what is heaven but a place where love is an eternal ecstasy, and where we can be lifted up above the tears and trials and loneliness of earth?

The beautiful is now understood as a quality which love bestows, and what is it but a reecho that humanity is beautiful to God because He loved it and gave Himself up for it? Love awakens to its messiahship and the realization that both partners are called upon to be the servants of life, as into their dual selfhood creeps a sense of their mission as the protectors and defenders of life. They may not know it, but their elemental instincts are rehearsals for a deeper love. Nothing transfigures love and lifts it to new heights as much as sacrifice, for love is freedom in search of servitude to another.

The only way that love is known is by an act of self-denial. There is much more of the divine in love than those in love know. First of all, they always speak of "our" love. "Our" love is more than the sum of the love of each. It is a reference to something outside of themselves of which they say, "This thing is stronger than we are." What is this love that is outside of them which pulls them together, except a reflection of that mysterious cycle of love in the very Heart of God? So long as the Divine is kept in marriage, there will never be cynicism. Every man will know that every woman promises him something that only God can give, and every woman will know that man promises her something that only the Divine can bestow. True love is really Divine Love on pilgrimage.

## *Going Steady and Early Marriage*

The problem of the age at which one is to marry is not absolute; it depends upon how mature spiritually and how mentally developed are the persons involved. To begin going steady at the age of fourteen or fifteen and to commit oneself exclusively to the other person is very much like buying a house when the foundations are laid. One does not know how many stories there will be, nor the size of each room, nor the arrangement of the floors. In marrying young, one does not make a choice of another partner; one just falls into a habit.

Such young people live under the illusion that they are in love when they are really only in love with an emotion.

The young must distinguish between liking and loving. The good-looking girl who passes any young man on the street produces on the fringe of his sensibility an impression; in fact, the girl probably makes far more impression on him than he does upon the girl, though this is hard for him to believe. The way her hair is tossed or her heels click in front of him creates a stimulus without his higher self ever having a part in it. If this results in an early courtship, there is a complete elimination of choice, due to this first attraction of the senses. When a man buys clothes, he does not always take the first suit offered him by the clerk, but a teenage suitor often does.

Going steady when young, with the first one who thrills emotionally, causes a *rigor mortis* in life. One sees it in the dress of many young teenagers. Once they start going steady or become engaged, they often no longer care how they dress or act in the presence of the partner. Why comb the hair? Why not wear dirty overalls on the street? They become like some women after ten or twenty years of marriage who never think of dressing well to please their husbands. Such teenagers are already in mental middle age.

The man that a girl loves at fifteen is not the one she will love at nineteen, that is to say, love enough to marry. Sometimes the one she loves at twenty is not the one that she would marry at twenty-three.

The reason is that a woman's nature cannot dissociate sex and love as readily as a man. Her nature is much more integrated, and her elements cohere more gradually. That is why a woman is slow to fall in love. She will not give herself until she completely possesses the personality or is ready to be possessed by the personality. This is the safeguard God has put into her to prevent her from making a fool of herself, like the little girl who recently bemoaned, "He broke off our engagement. He returned my frog."

## "Kicks"

A young mother ran away with five different lovers in five months, abandoning her children. She appeared before a judge who belonged to the new school advocating that compassion be shown to the criminal. The judge relieved the wife of the responsibility of her two children, allowed her to keep the home that she obtained in an original settlement with her estranged husband; he then allotted her $200 a month until she could get settled "emotionally." The judge, in concluding the case said, "She is more to be pitied than censured."

A Federal judge in Washington assailed what he considered to be "an unfortunate trend of judicial decisions which strain and stretch to give the guilty, not the same, but vastly more protection, than the law-abiding citizen." Bleeding hearts, some of whom are supposed to administer justice, are so concerned for criminals and terrorists that today the good citizens are considered off the reservation, as the new compassion exalts the guilty and condemns the innocent.

What is the cause of this reversal of judgment? The loss of a moral sense. Dostoevski wrote that in a future day men would say there is no crime, there is no sin, there is no guilt, there is only hunger; then men will come crying and fawning at our feet saying to us, "Give us bread." Nothing will matter except the economic.

A spirit of license makes a man refuse to commit himself to any standards. The right time is the way he sets his watch. The yardstick has the number of inches that he wills it to have. Liberty becomes license and unbounded license leads to unbounded tyranny. When society reaches this stage, and there is no standard of right and wrong outside of the individual himself, then the individual is defenseless against the onslaughts of cruder and more violent persons who proclaim their own subjective sense of values. Once my idea of morality is just as good as your idea of morality, then the morality that is going to prevail is the morality that is stronger. As it has been put:

> Pale Ebenezer thought it wrong to fight,
> But roaring Bill, who killed him, thought it right

Why is Satan so anxious to see the moral degeneracy of the West? Because it produces chaos, and chaos is the door the devil uses to enter and seize power. "When a strong man fully armed guards his palace, his possessions are safe," the Lord assured us. "So be vigilant. Be sure of this: if the master of the house had known the hour when the thief was coming, he would not have let his house be broken into." When a good shepherd sees his sheep begin to disperse, he sends a dog barking at their heels. Totalitarian regimes often arise out of the chaos created by license. The transition from "nothing matters," which is indifference to virtue and justice, to "everything matters," in which even our thoughts are controlled, is short and slippery.

Another effect of the growth of "everything goes" is a passion for more and more excitement. One notices that many juvenile delinquents state that they became drug addicts because alcohol no longer gave them a "kick." This is true of every sensation. To produce an equal effect or kick over a long period of time, one must increase the stimulus. One can get used to noise in a boiler factory. Weber and Fechner tried to tie up the psychological law with mathematics, stating that to increase the kick in the ratio of one, two, three, four, one had to increase the stimulus two, four, six, eight, sixteen. Now, after these delinquents have become used to drugs, what new thrill will be necessary? History proves that such emotionally exhausted individuals begin to be sadistic and take pleasure in inflicting cruelty on others. Could persecution of any social or religious class be in the distant future? It's hard to say. But this we do know, the policy of not restricting degeneration on the ground that it destroys freedom may lead to a love of seeing others punished to take the blame off ourselves. Even in television, the realistic and the possible already bore us; we must have the impossible, the supernatural. What faith! What credulity! Believing in the Resurrection of Divine Justice and Love demands less credulity and gives a thousand times more peace — and no demands for more violent kicks.

## The Curve of Love

Why is the curve of love chaotic? Should not love be a constant ascension — something like the indefatigable mountain climber who unerringly finds the peak? And yet the fact is: the curve of juvenile delinquency has increased eight hundred per cent. The United States has the largest narcotic market in the world.

Dr. Milton Senn, director of Yale's Child Study Center, states that of all marriages in which both partners were high school students, there was a premarital pregnancy in eighty-five per cent of the cases.

This brings up the question: are we suffering from a moral or a cultural degeneration? There is no doubt that we are suffering from a moral degeneration, but it involves more than youth. Therefore, we are also suffering from a cultural decay. It often happens that an individual who is frustrated may look for some kind of escape in sexual promiscuity. So it is with society. When it runs up against a dead end, many aberrations — artistic, political, economic and carnal — leave their sediment or scum on the surface of society.

Cultural decay reveals itself with society particularly in two areas: first in public life; second, family life.

In public life there is an evident want of integrity and honesty in such things as the primacy of the "fast buck," price fixing, built-in obsolescence in mechanical things, the substitution of the novel and the new for what is already practical and useful.

In family life, too, youth sees the wedding ring cut in two. Thirteen million youths in the United States are "half orphans." Some see drunken fathers, others see neurotic mothers. The want of fidelity and love in the home makes them despair as much of loyalty in private matters as of honesty in public.

Parents will often say in justification of their position, "I can do nothing with my children." This is an absolutely correct answer, but it needs an explanation.

A mother who takes drugs while she is carrying her child will see the child after birth suffer the effects of her own excesses. Somewhat the same symptoms of chills, "shakes" and other disorders pass into the infant. The mother, in the face of the victimized infant, may say, "I can do nothing for the infant." The fact is the mother has already done everything for the infant. She has made the infant that particular way. The blame is at her door, just as well as the blame for dishonesty and stealing in a boy is to be laid at the door of the father who cheated on his income tax.

Teenagers, when frustrated in these two important areas of life, look for some kind of escape, and these are generally twofold:

1. There is produced a generation of individuals who are actually in protest against culture. They ridicule everything because they have no confidence in it. This ridicule expresses itself in the way they dress or fail to dress, in a general uncleanliness by which they manifest that they feel themselves as strangers to society and are characterless in a characterless society.

2. The other outlet is the orgiastic, or the overemphasis on sex, in which the youth tries to escape the decay of society by a return to the primitive, seeking a release in blood, though he can never find it because he dresses it up in too sophisticated a manner. As a youth loves speeding not in order to arrive some place, but just for the excitement of speeding, so too a teenager is apt to turn to the carnal to make up for the loss of purpose of life and society and

family, by the intensity of an erotic experience. He seeks to destroy the mores which
he knows to be corrupt, and to drag everyone down to his own level. Abandonment
becomes a substitute for creativeness. He
hopes to recover some compensation for
what his sick soul has lost. Finding no home
for the soul in the world, he becomes self-
abandoned.

## The Proper View of Sex and Love

In the talk about sex today, there has been neglected
one profound relationship which the Scriptures
express, and that is the coordination of sex relationship and knowledge. This is the opposite extreme of
linking it up with animalism. Adam, for example,
"knew" Eve and she conceived. Mary said that she
"knew not" man. Why is knowledge used to express
the union of man and woman? It is because it is the
closest kind of union possible, namely, that between
the mind that knows and the thing that is known. It
is barely possible to distinguish oneself from what
one knows.

Just suppose a student never knew before that
Shakespeare was born in 1564 and died in 1616.

Once a professor communicates that knowledge to him, he will always be dependent on the teacher for that information. He can never put himself back into ignorance, though he may use the knowledge over and over again. So great is the student's relationship to a college for giving him an education, that the college is called the alma mater.

Sex is like knowledge for several reasons. First, it constitutes an intimate bond between man and woman, a union so close that it is like the mind and its knowledge. Furthermore, once the experience is entered into, just as in education, there is always a dependence upon the one who gave him the knowledge. This man has made her a woman, and this woman has made him a man. A two-in-oneness has been established, which can be repeated over and over again, but it can never be reacquired. The mind which learned a certain truth can never put itself back into ignorance; neither can one who has a knowledge of another put himself back into innocence. Stolen goods can be returned; harsh words can be taken back; a greedy man can repair his excesses by giving to the poor. But here a line has been crossed. The original has been destroyed. A bridge has been burned, and neither person can return again to what he or she was before this knowledge was acquired.

A further proof of this bond is to recall how often an unfaithful husband in search of extramarital experiences will practically always begin justifying his marauding with an intellectual position: "My wife does not understand me." If he wants to play another nine holes of golf, he does not invoke some rationalization such as, "My boss has an inferiority complex." But here the carnal masks itself with the spiritual, and the erotic with the intellectual. The truth is that the wife probably does understand her husband only too well. The second woman, in her turn, does not put the relationship upon a physical basis; she invokes her sympathetic and maternal instincts, which is another way of rationalizing her actions.

Sex is one of the means God has instituted for the enrichment of the personality. It should be properly seen as mirrored in that wider world of life. Love in monogamous marriage includes sex; but sex, in the contemporary use of the term, does not imply either marriage or monogamy. Sex seeks the part; love, the totality. Sex is rightly called a mystery. It has its matter in the physical powers of generation, and it has its form in its power to share in the creative purposes of God. Because sex is related to creativity and God is the source of all creativity, sex is seen to have an intimate bond with religion.

Sex, therefore, in its proper place, which is in marriage, is a summons from God to share in creation, since man and woman are God's co-workers in the sweet tasks of quarrying humanity.

## Obedience

This universe is governed by laws. Things are this way and not that way. By submission to laws we make them our own. For example, if we obey the laws of the body we keep it in health; if we obey the laws of the mind, we keep it learned. Spiritual being has its prizes too, as Our Lord said: "If you love Me, you will keep My commandments." In other words, true obedience springs from love, not from force.

The worst man in the world knows a great deal more of his duty than the best man does. It is not for want of knowledge that men go to pieces, but rather for want of obedience to the knowledge of the good they already possess.

Earthly rulers say nothing concerning the temper or spirit of those who obey; all they ask is compliance with edicts and laws. Threats and penalties are attached to infractions, such as a fine for speeding. The legal world says, "If you *fear* me, you will keep my commandments." But in the Divine order it is different. "If you *love* Me, you will keep My commandments."

In our day, liberty is taking the place of obedience. Obedience, it is said, has had its day. Civilization is in danger when the rights of liberty plead against the duties of obedience as if the two were opposed to one another. A man who has never obeyed is not the man who will know how to command. Steady drudgery and apprenticeship are the necessary training for the conduct of a great business. He will be a poor general who has never been a lieutenant in the ranks.

Hence Our Blessed Lord went down to Nazareth and was subject to His mother and foster father; then He became obedient unto death, even unto the death on the Cross.

Obedience is not the quality of slaves, for slaves act against their will. He who had liberty to do all things became subject to His parents to prove that obedience is the pathway to freedom. As St. Paul wrote to the Ephesians, "You who are children must show obedience in the Lord to your parents; it is your duty."

The parent is strong when he says to the child, "I must have your obedience because I am responsible to God for your upbringing in goodness and truth." On the other hand, the child's strongest encouragement is in the same thought: "In obeying my parents I am doing that which is pleasing to God, and I do it because I love the Lord."

In the book of Lamentations it is written: "It is good for a man to bear the yoke from his youth." A horse must be broken in while he is a colt; a dog must be trained when he is young. So it is with youth. He who has never learned to submit will make himself a tyrant when he obtains power. A silver spoon has choked many a youth.

St. Thomas Aquinas said, "The respect that one has for the rule flows naturally from the respect that one has for the person who gave it." Authority must always have behind it some value which elicits respect and reverence.

In courtship, there are no laws, but the lover always seeks to fulfill the will of the beloved; and in religion, no compulsion is felt by anyone who loves Christ. The real basis of obedience in the family, therefore, is not the fear of punishment, just as in religion it is not the fear of hell. Rather, it is based on the fact that one never wants to hurt anyone whom one loves. It will bear repeating that Our Blessed Lord said, "If you *love* Me, you will keep My commandments."

# THE PASSING OF YEARS

The popular song, "Time on My Hands," has far deeper significance than is generally envisaged. It could very well be that time is one of the greatest obstacles to happiness, and for two reasons.

Time makes the combination of pleasures impossible. Because we live in time we cannot simultaneously listen to Cicero, Demosthenes and Bossuet; because the clock of our life is wound but only once, we cannot at one and the same moment enjoy the snow of the Alps and the refreshing sunshine of the highlands of Kenya; because the heart beats out the lease on life, one cannot, despite the advertisements, "dine and dance" at one and the same time.

It is an interesting psychological fact that the more pleasurable are our moments, the less we are conscious of time. At the end of a pleasant evening with friends, or listening to good music, or being spiritually uplifted in prayer, we say, "Time passed like anything." When, however, work is a bore, visits a trial in patience and an appointment with the dentist a cross, time never seems to end. Hidden in this psychological and subjective judgment of the passing hours is already a hint of immortality and the necessity of a timeless existence in order to find perfect happiness. If the more we feel ourselves outside of time, the greater is our happiness, it follows that eternity is the one condition in which all things can be enjoyed at one and the same time. This, curiously enough, is the definition that the philosophers give of eternity: *tota simul*, all pleasures at once.

But in recent decades, with the decline of faith and belief in immortality, time has become one of the major causes of many psychotic and neurotic disorders. If there is no other life than this, if the daily burden of life leads to nothing more than the grave, if existence has no meaning, then time is the root of most of our anxieties. What then is life but a long corridor through which one passes closing doors, not knowing which door will be the last? Every crisis in life, every new turning in the road of existence, diminishes possibilities. The anxiety of the temporal then begins to press us down so that we are like a criminal awaiting a death sentence.

The passing parade of time, the slamming of the gates of opportunity, the calming of passions, forced retirements — all of these produce an existential anxiety which makes one wonder if it is worthwhile carrying on.

Because life does not end here, the closing of the doors of time and the burden of the years become bearable — because they lead to something better when properly utilized. That was why St. Paul said that for the sake of Christ he "gloried in his infirmities" and in his anxieties and in his sorrows. This was nothing but the continuation of the message of Our Blessed Lord: "Be not anxious." This means, "Have no existential anxiety about acquiring too much in time, for it ends and leads to judgment." So long as one lives for treasures that moths consume and rust eats and thieves steal, there is no possible escape from anxiety and worry. We cannot cast these cares upon God, for God has no interest whatever in making a person rich. As William James once wrote, "The sovereign cure for worry is religious faith. The turbulent billows of the fretful surface leave the deep parts of the ocean undisturbed, and to him who has a hold of vaster and more permanent realities, the hourly vicissitudes of his personal destiny seem relatively insignificant things." It is only to the extent that timeless existence, or eternity, is brought to bear upon all of our actions in time, that we become liberated from that awful, frustrating anxiety of the temporal.

## Indifference

Every teacher knows that it is easier to win a mind with a mistaken interest than one that has no interest at all. The greatest of the Apostles, Paul, came to the

Lord through the flames of hate, and the reason of his hate remained the reason of his love — a vivid recognition of all the Person of Christ stood for in relation to humanity. The sensuous passion of Magdalen finally swept in the opposite direction and became the supreme dedication of her love.

But what is extremely difficult for the blessings of heaven to work upon is indifference and the middle-age spread of false broadmindedness. The Lord can do something with the obviously bad, but it is rather difficult to do anything with the obviously good. They have outlived their hot venturesome days but have not yet seen into the vanity the world prizes. They are comfortable and hence ask for no change; because they have wealth, they think that they are worthful.

Tennyson in his "Holy Grail" tells the story of such a man, who surrendered all of his high ideals and settled down to a soft, materialistic, sensual life. Originally he had set off in search of the Holy Grail, but soon wearied of the quest; finding a silk pavilion in the field and merry maidens in it, he abandoned the search. Later on, when he returned to King Arthur's court, he ridiculed the idea of looking for that great and holy thing which the cup signified:

> It is a madness
> But by mine eyes and by mine ears I swear,
> I will be deafer than the blue-eyed cat

*And thrice as blind as any noon day owl,*
*To holy virgins in their ecstasies, henceforward.*

Dante in his description of hell said that when
he first entered it, he found some spirits that were
neither rebellious nor faithful, but existed solely for
themselves. They were "hateful, distasteful to God
and to His enemies."

When these indifferent souls steal, they do not
restore; when they have moral collapses, disgusting
to the moral sense, they do not repent, but creep
back into an old respectability; they judge themselves by the accepted standards of the group in
which they move; social refinement is regarded as
the flower and the aroma of virtue; secular conven-
tions are given the force of Divine commands; and
finally, they may call themselves stupid but never
sinful.

Herein lies the psychological reason for the
denial of immortality. Knowing that such indifference cannot escape judgment when all things are
weighed in the balance, they resort to denying it.
Shakespeare wrote:

*In the corrupted currents of this world,*
*Offence's gilded hand may shove by justice,*
*And oft 'tis seen the wicked prides itself*
*Buys out the law: but 'tis not so above;*
*There is no shuffling, there the action lies in His*
*true nature.*

No one can pick up the Scriptures without reading a devastating criticism of social moral standards, as when the Divine Savior put a harlot above a Pharisee, a penitent robber above a religious leader, a prodigal son above his exemplary elder brother. Many a tree as it stands in the forest looks fair, fine, solid and valuable, but when it is cut down and sawed for use reveals rottenness, cross grain and knots. Social conformity to low standards may give the appearance of goodness, but in the judgment of God the true character is revealed.

## Middle Age

One way of telling whether we are growing old is to revisit the college which we once attended. If the students seem "much younger" than when we were there, we are in middle age. Many alumni returning on the fifteenth or twentieth anniversary of graduation often say, "Today colleges are just filled with kids — much more immature than in our day." Someone meeting a policeman on the street remarked that today the policemen are much younger than when he was a boy. There actually has been no change in the age of the policemen; there is only a change in the age of the person speaking.

One of the best correlations of age and youth was made by Saint Augustine when he wrote, "Let your old age be childlike, and your childhood like old age; then your wisdom will not be with pride, nor your humility be without wisdom." Cicero wrote about many of the advantages of old age, one of which was that the passions become milder as we learn to run better in the harness. Life, as it goes on, expresses itself less in poetry and more in prose; enthusiasms fade away into a kind of impotent prudence. Some may feel they have left their passions behind, when actually it is the passions that have left them behind. They imagine that they have mastered life, when really habits which they cannot break have mastered and enchained them.

The German poet Schiller does not altogether share this idea. He contends that it is a physiological fact that the animal nature becomes more dominant over the spiritual nature in middle life, simply because body and soul are much more closely welded together than they were in youth. The passions indeed were stronger then, and more violent, but the moral nature also had a greater resiliency and could quickly bounce back to moral values. As physical recuperation was easier in youth, so too, unless there were gross excesses, spiritual or moral recovery was easier. The multiplication of bad acts which produce evil habits, the evil habits which produce the slaveries of sin, do not meet the resistance in middle age that they did during the elastic and more morally conscious attitudes of youth.

There seems to be some confirmation of this in Cardinal Newman, who states that the generalities of people of middle age have either sunk in heavy apathy, or else are more devoted to the mere material interests of life; these, when not counteracted, make a person selfish and indifferent to anything except his or her own comfort or profit.

In the more intellectual, this manifests itself in an indifference to any kind of moral or spiritual change; in the less cultured, or in the coarse and vulgar, it shows itself in a love for more violent excitement. It is particularly significant that one of the great passages of Dante is one in which he shows man encountering three animals: the fierce lion of wrath and pride; the sleek and many-spotted panther, who stands for lust; and the gaunt hungry wolf, representing avarice. All three he places in the middle region of our mortal life. Confucius said that human beings are governed by lust in youth, by pride in middle age and by avarice in old age. Whatever be the judgments, it is well for all of us to realize that we face a day of final reckoning, and we should say with Dryden:

> Already I am worn with cares and age;
> And just abandoning the ungrateful stage:
> Unprofitably kept at Heaven's expense
> I live a rent charge on His Providence.

## *Old Age*

Age has many purposes that are good and holy. The Old Testament makes old age the reward for obedience to parents. Saint Paul speaks of age as a merciful gift of Providence to enable us to do penance for the sins of youth. Age also becomes the fountain of wisdom and experience from which the young may drink. Michelangelo, who lived to be almost ninety, often used to repeat his motto as he chiseled marble that almost spoke: "I still learn." Cicero claimed that age gave stability to reason by the quieting of passions. Almost all fruits grow sweeter as they approach the time of plucking. Age is more merciful than youth. It was the young men who counseled David to be cruel; the old counseled him to be merciful. Those who have the faith and live virtuously dwell in radiant expectation of the glory that is to come.

And so one might go on enumerating the advantages of age as Cicero did in his work, *On the Old*. But here we come not to the subject of age, but rather, how rarely those who reach old age ever change from an earthly to a divine life. A famous Protestant preacher once said, "I have been twenty years in the ministry of the Gospel, and I do not believe that I could enumerate three persons over fifty years of age whom I have ever heard ask the solemn question: 'What shall I do to be saved?'" The Jewish prophet complained of his people, "Gray hairs are here and there upon him, and yet he knoweth not." This unconscious loss of life is pitiable, the approaching of the bar of justice and the refusal to set accounts in order.

Tempests are visible in their destruction; so are the violent outbursts of the passions of the young. But sometimes there is the dry rot which undermines all within; such is often the unrecognized deterioration of those who have lived in doubt, skepticism and faithlessness until the whole fabric collapses. The shutters of life were pulled down upon a heavenly city during youth and now there is not the strength to lift them. The real peril of age is that it may board windows that open on the Light and then claim that there is no light. Gray hairs are invoked as an authority on worldliness and godlessness, while a creeping paralysis leaves the soul untouched though "one rose daily from the dead."

There are three great passions in man which impel him to excesses in his desire for things that are good. These three are *lust*, which the modern world calls sex; *pride* or egotism; and *avarice* or greed, sometimes called security. Though they are not limited to any one generation, each has a tendency to be stronger in different periods of life. Flesh dominates youth. Egotism and struggle for power are apt to determine a man's middle age. Avarice, or greed, is generally the sin of old age. The piling up of money becomes a kind of immortality; by making himself secure in this life, one unconsciously believes he is procuring security for himself eternally. Youth is apt to be a spender; old age is more inclined to be a hoarder.

Such a life then becomes so materialized that there is never a thought of what is immoral or wrong. Rather there is a tendency to confuse having and being. Since he has worth, he believes he is worth. Indifference so possesses the soul that there is neither God nor Baal. As Francis Thompson put it:

> *So flaps my helpless sail,*
> *Bellying with neither gale*
> *Of Heaven*
> *Nor Orcus even.*

The best way to enjoy old age is to see in it a time for making up for the sins that went before, and living in hope for the joys that lie before one. But this takes Faith!

## Moral Landscapes

A person may say, "I am not as holy as I once was." This self-depreciation may, in some instances, be true, but there also may be considerable added enlightenment through the lapse of years. We become more humble and, therefore, more dissatisfied with ourselves; we pass through certain emotional stages and probably equate them with genuine holiness and with spiritual twinges. But may not this growing sense of imperfection be a sign of the perfecting of our spirit, in the sense that the faults once latent are now discovered? The clearer eye detects deformity and the finer ear the discords. It is very much like watching a sculptor at work; when he first touches the block of marble with heavy strokes he appears to mar the marble, and yet in the end a glorious statue rises under his hand. So the blows of God and the trials of life seem to spoil our ease; yet in the end, they work toward a beautiful harmony of spirit.

From a psychological point of view, there may be vain thoughts concerning the past. Distance has a softening power. Those things which appeared lovely at a distance cannot stand up before an immediate gaze. One of the great missionaries of the Middle Ages came to his vocation by following the sprightly walk of a young woman whom he saw on the street. He quickened his pace and finally caught up with her and spoke to her; when she turned her head, she revealed the face of a leper. It was this close view which inspired him to dedicate himself to the lepers and the poor.

Moral landscapes are something like physical landscapes; that is why we believe that in retrospect the rough has become the soft, and the harsh the sweet. It could very well be that the disgust with which men feel the shocks and buffeting of the generation in which they live makes them falsely conclude that past days were better. One notices this in the recently dead. How quickly the defects and the failings and even the vices of the dead seem to fade away with the passing of life. When friends and relatives were close to them, they saw faults. When they look at them now as those who have passed, all of the hidden goodness begins to appear.

One notices this in the stories of the saints of the Old Testament as compared with references to them in the New Testament. Those who were not too conspicuous as unblemished mirrors of sanctity, such as David, who committed adultery; Rahab; Moses, who killed a man; Abraham who lied twice about his wife — all of these are praised in the New Testament. It was the distance from their lives that, to some extent, added a luster which was not actually present during the days of the flesh. As one historian has put it, "The more carefully we examine the history of the past, the more reasons shall we find to dissent with those who imagine that our age has been fruitful of new social evils. The truth is that the evils are, with scarcely an exception, old. That which is new is the intelligence which discerns them, and the humanity which relieves them." Probably there are no new things happening in the world. There are only the old things happening to new people.

## Our Accountability

At the end of every day a slip is pulled out of a cash register, on which is written the debits and credits of the day's transactions. Each year the income-tax bureau reviews the statements of its citizens, making judgments on the honesty and dishonesty of their returns. The morning after excessive drinking, the head with its hangover makes a judgment on intemperance, as during the night the sick stomach passes judgment on the food that was not good for digestion. As audiences make judgment on a play by their applause, so there is to be a final accountability for the thoughts and the words and deeds of every human heart. In vain is it to be expected that we who pass judgment constantly on others should not pass in judgment ourselves.

It will be very difficult for us to give an account of others in strict justice, but in a general way we render more judgment on others than we do on ourselves. To judge others keeps us at the circumference of life and away from the center.

But there come moments, at night or when alone or in the silence of the country, where we cannot help but pass judgment on ourselves. But those whose consciences are no good avoid this by immersing themselves in externals. Hence the reluctance of such persons to be alone with themselves. They hardly ever enter into themselves, and partly because they have no center of personality. They search for constant distractions, or something "to make one forget," anything to keep the wound below the surface, and the memories from flying upward into consciousness

Even this very tendency to deny guilt or to suppress it, or to ridicule the fact of sin, is in itself a fear of judgment. No one is supposed to speak today of a man giving an account of himself to his Creator, any more than he is supposed to speak of cancer. And yet Daniel Webster was once asked, "What is the most important thought you ever entertained?" He replied, "My own individual responsibility before God."

Each man shall one day give an account of himself to God. Many do not want to hear about this; like Louis XIV, they do not wish death to be mentioned in their presence. All the veils which hide us from each other, or from ourselves, all the false excuses we have had for our sins, all the blame we thrust on Oedipus and Electra instead of ourselves — all these will drop away at the glance of the Divine eye. Nor will the accounting be arbitrary, capricious or external. It will be self-registering, automatic — we shall see ourselves as we really are. It is not the fact that God is going to judge us some day that is frightening; it is that our daily living is forging the judgment.

But here is the consolation: Scripture tells us of the dual role that Our Blessed Lord plays. He repeatedly affirmed that He was not on earth to judge the world, but to be its Redeemer, its Savior, its Advocate. Later on, He said, at the end of time, He would be the Judge of all men. This is the season of mercy; later, the winter of accounting.

A criminal rejoiced on discovering that his judge was once the attorney who defended him. But when the judge took his seat on the bench, he said to him, "When I was an attorney, I defended you, but I am no longer your lawyer. It is now not my business to defend. It is my business now to judge. I shall hear the evidence, but then I must deal with you in keeping with my oath of office."

While we are alive, Christ is our Advocate and Defense Attorney. When we come to the end of life and the great scroll is unrolled, then He becomes the Judge. To those who have lived well it will be like meeting a Judge Who is an old Friend, and from Whom we have nothing to fear.

# OUR NEEDS AND
# THEIR FULFILLMENT

## The Morality of Creaturehood

Certain built-in stabilizers keep human nature normal, as a governor in a motor prevents running it at excessive speed. No matter how much a man tries to make himself a god, there are limitations imposed upon him which remind him that he is a creature, not a creator.

The first of these is *sex*. Despite even a mad pursuit of erotic pleasure, every pursuer runs up against two dead ends: first, he is never able to possess completely the person who is loved; the partner always remains an unassailable fortress, a closed garden, a heart with its own thoughts and aspirations; second, even in the maddest pursuit of carnal ecstasy, the pursuer is always thrown back upon himself, alone and solitary. He started out to be a conqueror and he senses himself a victim. He plunges himself into an abyss where he hopes to be lost, but he floats again to the surface. He hopes to be absorbed in his new divinity, but like Baal, it falls apart. In fact, he is more lonely than before unless he accepts the other as a gift of God. Then joy reigns. Man is right in his pursuit of love; he is wrong in believing that the sparks he enjoys below have no flames from above.

The second limitation is *death*. Man is also hindered in making himself an absolute by the tragic fact of death. Baudelaire united the limitation of sex and the limitation of death by picturing Eros on a skull. Freud himself also united the two — sex and death. Even though the best of human love is more powerful than death, it seems to lead to death and thus becomes a paradox of human existence. A believer has an exit; the unbeliever, like Sartre, has no exit and, therefore, no hope. His *rigor mortis* sets in not at the moment of his physical death, but at the moment of his psychical death, when he fails to perceive the Resurrection behind the Calvaries of life. The realization of personality, the achievement of happiness, is impossible in the finite, limited created order. It presupposes the infinite, the eternal.

The third limitation is *knowledge*. One of the first questions asked by a child is "Why?" He tears apart his toys to find out what makes the wheels go around. Later on, he tears apart the toys of the universe to find out what makes them "tick." Though there is in man this infinite search for truth, he nevertheless bumps up against the wall: the more he studies, the less he knows. He finds new avenues of knowledge down which he might travel for a lifetime. It is only the self-wise man who thinks that he knows. The truly learned man, like Socrates, says that there is only one thing he knows, and that is that he knows nothing in comparison to the knowable.

There is a Divine urge toward life, which is

behind every meal, a love behind every sex drive, a truth which pushes the scientist into the laboratory and beyond. As we bathe in the rays of the sun, we do not always advert to the source of the light and the heat, but in the darkness and dampness, we know the sun is missing. He who knows there is perfect Life and Truth and Love, therefore, is never very much disappointed with the hurdles he has to meet in living and in knowing and in loving. But he who refuses to accept creaturehood as a limitation finds himself constantly frustrated. The gods he sought are tin. The staffs upon which he leaned have pierced his hands. In all anxiety, there is the unknown. In Truth, there is joy and peace.

## Taking the Mystery Out of Sex

In the previous article, we discussed the limitations imposed upon man which remind him that he is a creature, not a creator. In vain does one seek to escape these limitations by saying that the universe is characterized by nothingness. If this were so, why is this nothingness something that is feared, that haunts, that pushes victims onto psychiatrists' couches? As Hamlet said, it is this very dread of something after death which puzzles the will and makes us rather bear the ills we have than fly to others we know not of.

It may have been true that the Victorian era denied sex. But it may also be true that our day has gone to the other extreme. It has taken the mystery out of it. Parents have always felt that there was something about it that they could never communicate to their children. Rightly so. The physiology of it, yes. But the deep, personal relationship of husband and wife — that was invisible, incommunicable.

Sex today is no longer a mystery, inasmuch as it is currently reduced to a pure biological function. Because its mystery, which is a profound love for another person expressed in corporal unity, has been lost, the taboo on sex has disappeared. Sex in a human being is not the same as sex in a pig. Sex in a human is both a function and a communication. As a biological function, it is similar to that of animals. As a communication, it implies another person and is worlds apart.

Eros becomes meaningful when the purpose of the function is to become united with another person. Then it is quasi-divine. When that other person is seen as made in the image and likeness of God, the purpose of sex is the enrichment of personality, by and through another person.

A feeling of sadness, of frustration which comes from being hungry after one has eaten, or of being disgusted with food because it has not nourished, is like the frustration a personality feels in not being enriched by another. A wife is saddened at the humiliation of realizing that, as a person, she is not loved and that her role could be fulfilled by any other woman.

Sex as a function is replaceable, as one can substitute one pencil for another. Love is irreplaceable. No one can replace a wife, a mother or a father. Summoned by God, implanted by nature to be ushered into the mysteries of life, the woman is often condemned to remain on the threshold as a tool or an instrument of pleasure alone and not as a companion of love. Two glasses that are empty cannot fill up one another. There must be a fountain of water outside of the glasses in order that they may have communion with one another. There must also be outside of each a love wider and greater that binds them together. That is why lovers often speak of "our love" as if it were more than the sum of the love of each.

Sex as function may speak the language of love, but actually it is not the love of another person, but the love of self. The ego is put into another person in order to be loved. It is not the "thou" that is loved, but the "I" that is in the "thou."

Helmut Thielicke says the taboo has shifted from sex to death. "Nobody must tell the dying man that he must die, and funeral cosmetics put the mask of life on the corpse. Man can no longer cope with the finitude. He no longer knows how to fill this finitude with meaning, and therefore he must comfort himself with the pretense of a living corpse, the illusion of deathlessness; he is compelled to prolong an existence that remains unfulfilled. He tries to rub out the boundary line of death with lipstick."

The wolf offers nothing when he kills the lamb. Functional sex makes hungry where most it satisfies, for each person needs another person, and a person is a person only when seen as an image of God.

### The Apostolate of Reality

Francis Quarles has taken a view of beauty which seems a little base:

> *Gaze not on beauty too much,*
> *Lest it blind thee;*
> *Nor too near,*
> *Lest it burn thee.*
> *If thou like it, it receives thee;*
> *If thou love it, it disturbs thee;*
> *If thou hunt after it, it destroys thee.*

This view looks upon beauty as a temptress, and generally a bodily one. It forgets that beauty is more universal than tempting flesh. Beauty is nestling in the rosebud, walking like starry sentinels across the encampment of night, smiling in the cheek of a lily, rolling onto the surf in the measured harmonies of the wild waves. Beauty, when seen this way, is a gift, not a danger.

Everything beautiful in the world is a reflection of the Divine Beauty. As Augustine put it, "All that loveliness which passes through men's minds into their skillful hands, comes from that Supreme Loveliness, which is above our souls. For It my soul sighs day and night. From that supreme Beauty, those who make and seek after exterior beauty derive the measure by which they judge of it, but not the measure by which it should be used." For a long time in his life, he had failed to see that the beauty of earth was like a ray of the sun. When finally he traced back the beams of light to the great Furnace of Light, he cried out, "Late have I love you, O Beauty ever ancient, ever new, late have I loved you! You were within me, but I was outside, and it was there that I searched for you. In my unloveliness I plunged into the lovely things which you created. You were with me, but I was not with you."

One wonders if it be not true that of all the gifts that God gives, the one for which He receives thanks last and least of all is the gift of beauty. God gives wealth; those who receive it will often use it for holy purposes. God gives power of speech or music, and the gift is repaid in influence and song. But very often when beauty is given to a human being, the Good Lord gets back only old bones. One wonders if any mother ever thanks God for a beautiful child, or if a beautiful woman ever thanks God for the gift of beauty.

When human beauty is allied with virtue, then it becomes one of the most powerful means of an apostolate for Good. As Shakespeare put it:

> Oh, how much more doth beauty beauteous seem
> By that sweet ornament which truth doth give!
> The rose is fair, but fairer we it deem
> For that sweet odor which doth in it live!

"The beauty of the King's daughter is from within." Real beauty is from inside. An otherwise beautiful face is ruined by an ugly soul. That kind of beauty never makes anyone better; it becomes a rose to be trampled on. But the beauty of soul which shines through the prison bars of the flesh produces a hush of devotion and a spiritual admiration in others.

Beauty without virtue is like a fair flower that has an offensive odor. But true beauty bathes in that light without which nothing is beautiful. Beauty is a gift of God, like the rain. He allows the rain to fall upon the just and the wicked, and He gives beauty not only to the good, but even to the wicked. Wicked beauty strikes the eye, but the inner beauty of grace wins the soul.

## Temperance

Several decades ago there were many temperance societies. The term "temperance" was then almost always used in relationship to drunkenness, which very much narrowed the concept of temperance. Temperance really means self-control, or the ability to hold all of the faculties of mind, all of the instincts and movements of one's body in complete command, like the managed steed in the hand of the rider, or the helm in the hands of the steersman, or the plane under the mastery of the pilot. Someone has called it "that unvexed music of the body and soul."

The mind has two faculties: the intellect and the will. The intellect is the faculty of knowing: the will is the faculty of choosing. The intellect builds the target; the will shoots the arrows. One may have a target known to the intellect, but shoot the arrows astray because of a perverse will. Knowledge alone is no guarantee of virtue, because knowledge is a different power of the mind from the will. A learned person is not necessarily a saint. Nor is a saint or an individual of strong character necessarily learned. The knowledge we possess of things outside of us has little or nothing to do with our moral temperament.

William James, who wrote many wise things about psychology, said of character being in the will, "The strong-willed man is the man who hears the still, small voice unflinchingly, and who, when the death-bringing consideration comes, looks at its face, consents to its presence, clings to it, affirms it, and holds it fast, in spite of the host of exciting mental images which rise in revolt against it, and would expel it from the mind. Sustained in this way by a resolute effort of attention, the difficult object before long begins to call up its own congeners and associates and ends by changing the disposition of the man's consciousness altogether."

Temperance does not mean not drinking, not eating or not enjoying God-given instincts. It is rather the controlling of these excellencies in order that they may not run into faults. Some edible plants, for example, if they are allowed to go to seed, can poison a person; so one's good qualities need to be kept under order, so that they be not exaggerated into weakness. As long as we remain masters of our affections and desires, we can live in peace. It is a bad job when the fire extinguisher catches fire, and that is exactly what happens when our will through abuse becomes so weak that we are unable to be master of our own fate and destiny, but become bribed and enslaved. The drunken Rip Van Winkle portrayed by Joseph Jefferson excuses himself for every fresh dereliction by saying, "I won't count this time." He may not count it, but the eternal registers count it, and it is being counted in the nerve cells and fibers of his body. Napoleon once said of Ferdinand of Spain, "He is a man incapable of governing himself, and of course he is incapable of governing the peninsula."

An athlete on the field or a boxer in the ring will do better because encouragement is shouted at him. But in building a self-controlled character, the loneliness of a struggle makes it the harder. There is no audience to encourage us; hence, a powerful spiritual motive is required. Here is a battle that is not being watched, except by God and the self. The fact that God is watching prevents us from evil, but more important still is the fact that we may also call upon Him for strength.

## Character

A normal human being is one in whom all of the emotions are subject to right reason, to conscience and to the law of God. No emotion can completely possess us until reason evaluates and the will allows it its free sway. In a normal household, a person may allow his own dog to come up the stairs into the house, but he will not allow all the dogs in the neighborhood to follow. That would be irrational.

Right reason suggests eating food sufficient for health, but not eating food enough for ten. Right reason tells us that we ought to allow enough light to come to our eye in order to read, but right reason would not recommend the eye's looking into an ultraviolet arc. Right reason suggests putting the ear within reach of harmonies, but not within the reach of an explosion.

A radio station once received a letter from a man who asked them to strike the note A on a studio piano. He told them that he had an old fiddle which was out of tune, and all the pleasure he got out of life was playing his fiddle. The man was affirming that there is a standard to which he must conform. Right reason, conscience and the law of God are that standard for all the emotions.

We live in a vale of character-making, and character is made by bringing the complexities of emotional life to unity under right reason and morality. As long as emotions are held on the leash of goodness and truth and moral law, there are character, happiness and self-possession. There are those who say that there is "nothing wrong with sex." This is correct, if by sex is meant the expression of one's love which is open to the propagation of the human species according to right reason and the moral law. But the statement could be wrong if it meant that sex is never capable of excesses and deordinations. The emotions without right reason become like rivers without embankments.

It is also argued that all of our instincts are right, and therefore should be obeyed. But it must not be forgotten that our human instincts are subject to reason, and therefore are to be rationally and morally guided. A man has a hunting instinct just as a fox does, but it is not rational for husbands to hunt mothers-in-law. It is also argued that if young people knew the evil effects of the excesses of sex, and were told of their consequences, they would have no urge to abuse sex, just as they would have no urge to go into a house where there was a quarantine sign. The argument is fallacious, first of all, because such a position fosters only hygiene and not character; secondly, it does not make allowances for every individual's believing that he will escape the evil effects. More important still, it forgets that no young person has an urge to break down a door on which a quarantine sign is written, but everyone has a sex urge, which needs considerable control.

Too much emphasis is laid upon the fact that we must adjust ourselves to our environment and adjust ourselves to society. Rather, we must be self-adjusted, by subordination of body to soul, senses to reason, reason to faith. Actually there is a decline of the right kind of passion and enthusiasm due to a want of the love of truth.

## Great Moments of Decision

Napoleon held that the fate of every battle was decided in the space of about five minutes. All the maneuvering and all the preparations led up to the strategic moment of crisis. If the leader had vision to take advantage of those few moments, the enemy's rout would be complete; if, however, he allowed it to pass, defeat was certain. In one battle his forces were halted before a bridge over a deep ravine. If the bridge were not crossed, the battle would be lost. The soldiers were afraid to advance upon it inasmuch as it was swept by the fire of Austrian cannons. Napoleon snatched the flag from the standard bearer and rushed onto the bridge shouting, "Forward to save your general!" The effect upon the soldiers was electric and in that five minutes the battle was decided.

It could very well be that the life of every person is not so much decided by the routine events of every day, but rather during two or three great moments of decision which happen in every life. As Shakespeare put it:

> *There is a tide in the affairs of men*
> *Which taken at the flood, leads on to fortune;*
> *Omitted, all the voyage of their life*
> *Is bound in shallows and in miseries.*

If the opportunity is allowed to slip by unimproved, success turns into failure. There is the name of a place which signifies such a turning point in the lives of men and that is Kadesh Barnea, which is situated on the southern border of the Promised Land. There came a point in the pilgrimage when the children of Israel were within striking distance of their inheritance. They sent out spies, twelve of them, to report on the land they were about to take. The majority report, made by the representatives of ten of the tribes, was that the land could not be taken because the cities were too fortified and the enemy too numerous. The minority report, brought in by Joshua and Caleb, was turned down despite the fact that God had told the people through Moses that they would possess the land. It was this point in the journey, like the five minutes in the battle, which determined their future. With the fruit of their tribulations within their grasp they refused to take it and thus had to continue wandering in the desert for many years.

There is a Kadesh-Barnea in every nation, a critical moment when it has the power to turn back a force from without, or a corrosion from within. It has been called "a time of visitation" when power is given to vanquish, but if not seized, turns the nation into a kind of cadaver on which the scavengers feed.

There is a Kadesh-Barnea in every individual's spiritual life. One's background may have been filled with unbelief, guilt, dishonesties, adulteries and any of the seven pallbearers of the soul. Then there comes a moment of illumination to the mind, perhaps in a moment of sickness or a startling thought while reading, or the vision of innocence in a child. If this grace is responded to, a person is lifted out of himself, cuts connections with the past and starts out on a new career and new paths, with Heaven shining in his face.

All too often we play with opportunity as a toy, and when our eyes are opened to see its value, lo! it has vanished. Many of us reach the margin of a glorious destiny and then turn back to the desert. The path of duty, in a flash of the eye, becomes very plain, but self-indulgence makes the soul as blind as a mole. Were we to deal honestly with these pious inclinations and whisperings of conscience, we should see through the thin guise of our own pre-tenses and would strip the veneer of insincerity from our deeds. There is often a conspiracy in all of us which works against ourselves; we hunt for excuses to cover up our disobedience, but in a single moment, our life can be changed — not by pulling ourselves up through the power of our own will, but by a response to Heaven's inspirations which leaves the deserts of the world behind.

## Encounter with God

Men and women today do not come to God through the order of the universe; they come to Him through disorder within their own selves. The argument is still valid that the Heavens do declare the glory of God, but we rarely see the stars, and neon lights hardly reflect anything. When men could see nature, they argued back to nature's God. In the complexity of modern civilization man, however, sees himself less as living in nature, but more as living within himself.

It must not be assumed that it is only through the order and finality of the universe that one comes to the Creator; one can also come to the knowledge of the light through shadows. Health is more often appreciated after a sickness. Modern man has many encounters with God, but he does not know that he has met God. His encounters with God may come in a moment of disgust or sickness, after some kind of excess, or in a holy desire to be like another person who spends himself and is spent on his neighbor, or it may be through a pious inspiration.

These encounters or soul skirmishes do not necessarily mean that one begins to know God. Jacob wrestled all the night without knowing who his opponent was until the break of day. The young man who was born blind was questioned by the Pharisees as to who it was who cured him. He answered, "Whether He is a sinner I do not know. One thing I do know, that whereas I was blind, now I see."

The woman at the well who was living in adultery did not know immediately Who it was Who confronted her at midday at the well. She first thought Him to be a Jew, then a gentleman, then a prophet, then a messiah, but only at the end did she recognize Him to be the Savior of the World.

One of the most common encounters is in the moment of emptiness, boredom or fed-up-ness. This comes generally after a sensible pleasure or a mood of exaltation, as when the bills come into the kitchen when the honeymoon is over. It is an hour of need, and every need cries out for fulfillment. The need may be compared to a hollow space that rattles as it cries out to be filled; every void is related to a desire, a groping, a reaching out, a yearning for something.

This need can be multiplied, such as food for

the stomach, learning for the mind, companionship for the heart. But whatever it be, it has one basic characteristic: *The longing cannot be stilled by our own power, but with the aid of another.* There is need of some extraneous agent to fill up the cavity. The individual himself feels impotent and powerless. Associated with this need is what a distinguished Viennese psychiatrist, Dr. Igor Caruso, has called "the need of salvation." The One Who can enter is God, but there is no one who can force Him to enter. The human person can bar the doors to the Divine Visitor

It is here that one comes face to face with the problem of existence. The well-known Jewish psychiatrist, Dr. Viktor Frankl, who passed through two concentration camps, one Nazi, the other Communist, had ample evidence to study the findings of meaning and purpose, even in trial. Some turned a deaf ear to the encounter with God and of them he writes, "Often, existential frustration leads to sexual compensation. The sexual libido often becomes most rampant in an existential vacuum." Others, he said, became religious through this encounter, and he defines a religious man as "one who actually does not feel responsible to something, but to someone." From that point on, one learns he can endure any "how?" in the world, because he knows the "why?" — namely, that all things compensate unto good to those who are called to fulfill their need of salvation.

# THE NATURE OF OUR MINDS

Every human being at his birth has everything to learn. His mind is a kind of blank slate on which truths can be written. How much he will learn will depend on two things: how clean he keeps his slate and the wisdom of the teachers who write on it.

The cleanliness of the slate is dependent upon the way he lives, i.e., his moral life. It is too often assumed that ignorance is due solely to a want of learning. This is not true. Not every Ph.D. is a saint. An evil life prevents the accumulation of wisdom.

The human mind has two faculties: one speculative, which is directed to knowledge; the other the will, which carries that knowledge into action, and which chooses and decides. An evil life does not spoil the speculative intellect. An atomic scientist who is immoral does not directly impair his atomic knowledge. But when it comes to judgment, to directing and guiding, then the evil life exercises its influence. Any person who consults a psychiatrist should first make an analysis of the kind of life he lives, because though his scientific equipment may be good, when it comes to giving counsel, the doctor may be incapable. Our Blessed Lord warned that behavior affects attitudes toward Him. "You will not come to Me because your lives are evil."

The second condition of learning depends

upon the nobility and wisdom of the teachers. Teachers exist on three levels. We may learn from *nature alone*, which makes us scientists; or from *others*, which makes us humanists or intellectuals; or we may learn from *God*, Who alone can give us wisdom.

Almost all of us are willing to learn, either from the book of nature, or from the lips of others. But some of us are unwilling to accept mysteries or the revelation of God, or wisdom which transcends both the power of nature and the learning of others.

Mystery, however, does not mean an idea which is opposed to reason, but one which transcends it. Mystery is like a telescope of the eye. The instrument does not destroy vision, but opens new worlds hitherto unrevealed. A proud person might ask why he or she should believe that there is anything else in the world to see or know, except that which one's natural powers can compass. Pride then precludes the knowledge of other worlds.

G.K. Chesterton once said that God has put a tremendous mystery in nature itself and that is the sun. In the light of that one thing, which we cannot see because of its brightness, everything else is made clear. Likewise, though we cannot comprehend the nature of God completely in this life, nevertheless, in the light of the truths which He revealed, everything else is made clear, such as the mystery of pain, suffering, death, life and birth.

There are, therefore, two kinds of wisdom: wisdom of the flesh and the wisdom which God gives. One is very often opposed to the other. The first would say this is the only life there is; therefore, we should get all we can out of it. The other sees that this life is a kind of scaffolding up through which we climb to eternal happiness; it will, therefore, be so used as a ladder to the Mansions of the Heavenly Father. But this Divine Wisdom comes only to those who have qualifications for receiving it, and, as was pointed out above, one of the first conditions is good behavior. As Our Blessed Lord said, "If any one will do My Will, he will know My doctrine."

Crisis produces a hardened spiritual feeling which hinders understanding. Men do not like what they do not understand, or that which would demand a change in their lives. All the training of a university will not make certain persons mathematicians. If a person does not love truth and honesty, he cannot be made truthful and honest by expounding the definitions of these virtues. One must begin by creating within him conduct along the lines of these virtues; then he can be taught.

## *Legion*

One wonders if modern psychology has ever found a word which so adequately describes an unhappy and disturbed personality as the word legion. The word is found in the description of the mad man of the Gerasenes, who when asked by Our Lord to describe himself answered, "My name is Legion: for we are many." Notice the contradiction between my and we. He did not know what he really was, except that he was tossed about hither and thither by a crowd of wild and disordered impulses.

A disordered soul is characterized by the same sort of thing that has happened to an atom, namely, fission. Everywhere there is a breaking up, an alienation, a fragmentation and a dissolution. Such a person no longer is a unit. He is divided first within himself; he is divided from his fellowman; he is alienated from God.

Modern art, which is so expressive of the times, rarely paints a man such as one sees on the street. In one of the classic paintings of modern man, he has only one eye; the rest of him is made up of squares, cubes, cross lines and meaningless figures all combining to indicate complexity, diversity, tension, multiplicity and chaos. Every now and then a good thought may cross such a mind, but it has no roots. It is like magazines which editorially plead for a more disciplined youth and then on the other pages do everything, through pictures of excesses and merry carousing, to destroy it.

There are certain conflicts and tensions which are natural to us as human beings, namely, the conflict between the flesh and the spirit. In the young it is not always clear which is dominant or will be the master during life. It takes a lot of struggle to give dominance to the higher part of our being. For that reason, an artist refused to paint the portrait of a young man. The artist said that he saw two impulses in the youth neither of which yet showed dominion. He would delay the portrait until his character was formed.

But over and above that basic tension, there is the divided personality which comes from bad behavior. Such souls feel like Emile, who twice wrote in his journal, "My name is Legion," adding, "Reflection comes to no useful end, because it is forever returning upon itself, disputing and debating: I am wanting in both the general who commands, and the judge who decides." Modern literature has many descriptions of this "foreign legion" — disrupted, agonized souls who are alien to themselves. Albert Camus calls man a stranger because he has no permanent relatedness to anything, either fellowman or God.

There are many who do not realize this complexity in their lives. The moment they do, they begin to come close to God, Who alone can restore order and unity. When Our Lord restored the personality of the young man, He uttered a command which assumed that there was an intruder in his spirit. He ordered the evil spirit to depart.

There are three spirits which may govern the human heart: the spirit of the world, the spirit of evil and the Spirit of God. There is no disharmony caused by the first two that cannot be turned into a melody of joy by the Spirit of God, which is beyond the human and the psychological. When it is recognized that nothing so splits a man as sin, then immediately it becomes clear that nothing so much harmonizes a man as the Savior.

## Enthusiasm

Hearts would save themselves many sorrows if they knew better the psychology of human feelings. While there is much wisdom in the counsel of Emerson, "Hitch your wagon to a star," and to the need of wedding idealism to every ordinary task, there must also be a realization that enthusiasms cool. Those who have been to the North Pole say that the ecstasy at reaching it was very much dampened by the long, weary Arctic winter, during which the hidden weaknesses of men begin to appear. As fires died down, quarrelsomeness stole in.

Three laws may be given to help judge the difference between true and false enthusiasm:

1. Decisions and resolutions taken during an enthusiastic moment mean little unless tested by time and by waiting. At the beginning of the public life of Our Lord, when many wished to follow Him, He refused to accept them: "He knew what was in man." The immediate request for places on the right and left side of the kingdom by James and John He ordered tested by the ability to bear sacrifice and to drink the cup of His Passion and His Crucifixion. When, after multiplying the bread, the multitude wished to make Him a bread king, Our Lord fled into the mountains alone. Economic kingships last only while the bread is plentiful and the circuses are in the playgrounds. It is always a good policy never to choose the most enthusiastic person in a gathering as a leader. Wait to see how much wood there is for the flame.

2. Almost all moments of high sensible exaltation are followed by a period of depression. This is particularly true in any experience which has to do with the flesh. Drunkenness is followed by the hangover, excesses by

disgust, the dream stage of opium by disenchanting depression. The body cannot sustain continued pleasure. Even tickling can turn into pain.

3. In all human love it must be realized that every man promises a woman, and every woman promises a man, that which only God alone can give, namely, perfect happiness. One of the reasons why so many marriages are shipwrecked is because as the young couple leave the altar, they fail to realize that human feelings tire and that the enthusiasm of the honeymoon is not the same as the more solid happiness of enduring human love. One of the great trials of marriage is the absence of solitude. In the first moments of human love, one does not see the little hidden deformities which later on appear. It is not the great hurts which cause enthusiasm to cool, but rather the steady diet of mediocrities, the repeated insincerities, the getting used to one another's company, the everyday dust of human existence. There comes a moment when the wife seems less beautiful just because of the habit of seeing her. What is often seen is no longer thought to be beautiful. Much of what is beautiful is determined by two things: by surprise and

by love. When enthusiasm cools, then one hears, "You are not the one whom I married."

It is not to be thought that life is a snare or an illusion because the bubbles cease in a champagne glass. No true unhappiness comes to man unless he places his heart in a false infinite. He who sees that all human love is nothing but Divine Love on pilgrimage will use it as a kind of Jacob's ladder to climb back again through virtue to the Source of all Love Which is God Himself. Such spiritual fires never cool, because they are not fed by glands, but glow with the coals lighted at the furnace of Heaven, such as touched the lips of the prophet. Many of the false enthusiasms in the world today come from unhappy minds in unhappy bodies. They find a spurious happiness in setting destructive fires, burning down the temple of worship and the home of morality. The truest enthusiasms and fires are never loud. Our Lord's voice was never heard shouting in the streets, yet He came "to cast fire upon the earth." To be enthusiastic in that case is to live out the meaning of the word, for enthusiasm comes from two Greek words meaning to be in God.

## *Depression*

One of the better known psychiatrists of the world reports the following case of depression in a victim of tuberculosis. The psychiatrist sent the patient to the mountains, confined treatment to medication and the routine psychotherapy which all such doctors use in depression. The patient did not improve, so the psychiatrist questioned the medical superintendent as to whether or not there was any correlation between the tuberculosis and the low spirits of the patient.

The doctor in charge of the sanatorium answered, "I am convinced that if one went systematically into the psychic antecedents of our inmates, one would find that in at least half of them a depressive phase preceded the development of their tuberculosis." The psychiatrist then proceeded on the basis of working up a synthesis of the physical and the mental states and found that because of a mutual lack of understanding, the patient's marriage was about to go on the rocks. Being weak-willed, he filled the void by "playing around" with others.

The wife, discovering it, withdrew more into herself while the husband got farther from the wife by liaisons with others. In turn, the wife was further alienated from her husband because of the injury received.

Further analysis revealed that the patient had fallen first a victim to psychic depression and then, a year later, to tuberculosis. The idleness in the mountain lodgings only increased the depression of the patient. A cure was finally effected by a double technique, that is, giving work to the patient which was commensurate with his strength, and also through religion, to establish a moral reformation in his life and the breaking of evil attachments. The psychiatrist reports the double cure of depression and tuberculosis.

Doctors today note an increasing correlation between moral health and physical health, between our flight from responsibility and the despair which comes with irresponsibility. But this area remains within the practice of medicine and psychiatry. Our point here is to indicate rather the spiritual, moral and psychological reasons for depression. A frequent cause is rebellion against forces over which we have no control, such as sickness, loss of fortune and bereavement. Some sufferings cannot be alleviated. St. Paul, for example, had what he called a "thorn in the flesh." No one knows precisely what this thorn was, whether it was an affliction of the eye or of the body, or of enemies, or of false friends. In any case, three times he asked to have it removed and received the answer, "My grace is sufficient for you."

Acceptance, here recommended to Paul, was quite different from resignation. Resignation is passive, namely, a gritting of one's teeth and a bearing with it. Acceptance, however, is active, such as the prayer of Our Lord in the Garden: "Not My Will, but Thine be done." Accepting suffering and disease and bereavement does not mean taking pleasure in them or steeling oneself against them, or hoping that time will soften them. It means offering them to God so that they can bring forth fruit.

One psychiatrist tells of visiting a patient and saying to him in the midst of his suffering, "You know that the most important thing in this world is not to understand, but to accept." With a happy smile he answered, "Yes, it is true, I do accept — everything." During the night he fell asleep but suddenly awoke, the psychiatrist reports, and said aloud, "I am going to Heaven," and then passed away.

It is not, however, easy to acquiesce in the slow march of Divine purposes. Life is short, and everyone would like to reap the harvest and not leave it to another generation before death seals his eyes. Reformers and idealists are constitutionally impatient and are indignant with their fellowman for his sluggishness, and with God for His majestic slowness and unrevealed purposes. But there is deep truth in the paradox that if we hope for what we do not see, then with patience we wait for it. It is uncertainty which makes earthly hope short of breath and impatient of delay.

True acceptance, on the contrary, is based upon this hope, that the trials and sufferings of this life not only can be used for making up for our sins, but also can be applied to bring them to God. Recently there died in New York City a well-known man in the athletic world. Being told that he was dying of cancer he wrote to two of his friends who had abandoned their faith and told them that he was offering his sufferings for their intentions that they would return and make peace with God. Every person with faith knows that he receives fewer blows than he deserves. One man in affliction, when asked how he bore it, answered, "It lightens the stroke to draw near to Him Who handles the rod." When there is much rust upon our lives, then there is needed a rough file. In any case, one never complains. Christ is the best Physician; He never takes down the wrong bottle.

## Self-Pity

It has been my lot to spend much time with men who have suffered in prisons, death marches, Siberia, concentration camps and other forms of Communist tortures. But I have never known any one of them who ever said a harsh word against his persecutors. Like some trees which bathe with perfume the ax which cuts them, they had nothing but pardon for those who did them violence. They hated Communism, but they loved the Communists.

On the other hand, I have known people in very pleasant circumstances in an affluent civilization who could not stand being crossed. They were sensitive to the least verbal criticism or barbed dart of ill-feeling, hating not only the person but the cause for which the person stood. Because they did not like the looks of the captain of the ship, they were ready to jump overboard.

Why is there so much joy in the first group and so much sadness in the latter? It is because the first group has pity on others, while the second has self-pity. When Our Lord was being led out to Calvary, the pious women came to console Him, but He addressed them saying, "Weep not for Me, but weep for yourselves and your children." In other words, "Your pity is misplaced. It is not for Me that you should mourn, but rather weep for those who send Me to death. Shed no tears for the Crucified, but for the crucifiers. I go to a momentary sorrow, but there is a glorious Resurrection issuing from it. In every flame there is a point of quietness and repose where a match may be inserted without igniting; so too within My heart, already so crowned with the thorns of sorrow, there is an oasis of joy which no man can take from Me."

The self-indulgent, on the other hand, always find fault with others. The blame has to be placed somewhere: the boss, the nagging wife, the teachers, the politicians or the nasty man at the next desk. The sense of justice is so rooted in the human heart that responsibility must be laid on some shoulders; if not on self, where it belongs, then on another, where it does not. The self-pity awakens a sorrow which leads to despair and remorse.

Take the other case of those who suffer unjustly but with faith and love of God in their hearts. They may have a sadness in their hearts from pain and torture, but never remorse. They end in penitence or a making up for guilt by bearing patiently the trials of others. This is illustrated in the case of Judas and Peter. There is much similarity between the two, up to a point. Our Lord warned both of them that they would fall; He even told them that each would be a devil.

Both did deny the Master and both repented or were sorry. But the Greek word used in the Scripture is not the same in both instances. Judas repented unto himself — he had self-pity. Peter repented unto the Lord — he had penitence, sorrow and a desire for amendment. Peter cleaned the weeds out of the garden, but Judas killed the nocturnal brood of remorseful serpents in his breast by hanging himself.

Suppose one took a paper and wrote down the

number of times he succumbed to the vice of self-pity in a day. What a catalog of egotism it would be and what a revelation of character. On another page, one could write down those who were blamed for what was really our own fault. It could make one penitent, which means recognizing that the root of all our trouble lies within ourselves. How much do my neighbors have to put up with because of me, and how often does my egotism stand in the way of brotherly affection on their part? But a more serious question is: how often does this self-pity stand in the way of God's doing anything for me? I have so blocked up the cave of my mind that no light can enter. When the Master says to our Lazarus' soul, wrapped in the trappings of egotism, "Come out," we say, "No, I want to stay here in the grave of my inner discontent."

Nothing so blocks happiness and peace in the soul as a pampered ego. So much of what men call atheism is not so much the negation of God as the deification of the ego. Every atheist believes in God, but the god is himself. Being surrounded with so many limitations, frustrations and weaknesses, he develops more and more a hatred for the God Who is the Shepherd seeking lost sheep among the brambles. No wonder there are so many atheists today. It is hard to believe that each of them is a god. To accuse ourselves before the God Who took upon Himself the sins of the world is to move from self-pity and despair to the area of pardon and mercy. There is one thing worse than sin — denying that we are sinners. But there is hope in that, for unless we sinned, we could never call Jesus "Savior."

## Dreams

Our flights from reality may be either conscious or unconscious. They are conscious when one wills to become an alcoholic to forget. But flights may also be unconscious, as in dreams.

Everyone knows the theory of Freud which holds that every movement or false step or wrong word is a betrayal of some secret or unconscious opposition to what is conscious. The subconscious in these cases is trying to sabotage and wreck what is conscious. Psychiatrists give the example of a young man whose father and mother were never interested in him; the father was interested in business, and the mother in bridge. The young man then attached himself to another young man who was a homosexual. The young man, whom we will call John, then became a kind of defenseless victim of his friend. They would go motorcycle riding together with foxes' tails flying from their hats or from their handlebars, but all the time John was anxious to break this liaison which made him so unhappy and despairing. One day while John was driving the motorcycle with his friend on the rear seat, he ran into a tree. The psychiatrists say that John was betrayed by his subconscious into a violent solution of the problem.

No one has disputed Freud's basic idea that dreams are a meaningful psychic phenomenon, but his particular interpretation has been very much disputed, namely, that many dreams are repressed desires and particularly those of the libido, or sex. By 1914 several of his closest workers, including Carl Jung, Alfred Adler, Wilhelm Stekel, Otto Rank and others, broke with him because of the narrowness of his interpretation. Jung held that the dream was a kind of thermostat in the human system, or something that maintained equilibrium or balance. It was a compensating factor for many aspects of a problem which were either overlooked, undervalued or suppressed. Just as sweating is a compensation for being too hot, and panting is a compensation for excessive beating of the heart, so too the unconscious has to compensate for the excesses in its consciousness. With Jung there is less desire to explain dreams by infantile aspirations than with Freud, and more relatedness to adult life.

An example of the compensatory nature of dreams is the rather common dream that egotists, boasters and braggarts often have about falling. In their own conscious life they are always running the danger of having their thoughts discovered, and the dream strikes the balance of humility against the lie of pride. The dream is a compensation for a deficiency in the person and is, according to Jung, a revelation of his spiritual state.

Jung gives another interesting example of compensation in dreams. It is concerned with a woman who was proud of her intelligent, deep understanding of psychology, and who had recurring dreams about another woman. Whenever she met this other woman, she disliked her and thought her to be an intriguer, dishonest and vain, but in the dream the woman appeared always as a sister, friendly and likable. The intelligent woman could not understand why she should dream so favorably about a person she disliked. Jung said that the dreams were attempting to convey to her the idea that she herself was "shadowed" by an unconscious character that resembled the other woman. The dream was actually telling her about her own pride and power complexes, which completely misjudged other people. It was this sophistication of hers which made her so very unpopular in everyday life with her friends. She was blaming her friends in waking life, and the dream revealed that the friends themselves were blameless and nice; it was she who was ugly and nasty.

Not all dreams would fit into this theory of

Jung's, but there is no doubt that it would be useful to examine our dreams to find out what we are hiding, what we fear and what we really are. Dreams may occasionally hold a "moment of truth."

## Religion Has Moved to the Subconscious

We live in what might be called the Age of Bad Conscience. We cover it up by denying responsibility; we find scapegoats; we attack religion and all who have to do with conscience as if their extinction might give us immunity from that distinction between right and wrong. If any science is unpopular today it is certainly theology, particularly when couched in the language of reason and concepts which are alien to our moods and frustrations. But this does not mean there is no religion in modern man. There is; but it has moved from the area of conscience to the subconscious.

We say "religion" because nothing that is in man escapes the Providence and Mercy of God. It is just as easy for God to work in a cellar as a first floor, as well in the realm of emotions as in the realm of reason. The very uneasiness of the subconscious mind with its fears and dreads and anxieties is a kind of chaos for what might be called an anti-peace. But this chaos might be likened to the chaos in the second verse of Genesis, when the first creative word was rejected and left nothing behind but disorder. And over that chaos the Spirit hovered like a dove bringing order out of the disorder of creation, as the Holy Spirit, later on, breathing over Mary, brought order out of the chaos of humanity.

God speaks more frequently through our sub-conscious mind, probably, than through our conscious mind, simply because our self-consciousness puts up obstacles to Him. God can guide us quite naturally in a particular direction without our being aware of it. What was it, for example, that induced Paul Claudel, an agnostic and unbeliever, to enter Notre Dame Cathedral at midnight on Christmas, and ultimately to receive the gift of faith? Here was a reasonable man who was guided unreasonably. Very often stupid people come to God through very reasonable arguments, and reasonable people come to God through no argument at all.

There is an outward force operating on the subconscious mind which changes its direction. If a ball is thrown across a room, it will go in an unhindered path unless a foot or a hand is put out to divert it. The subconscious mind may be governed once by vice, and then suddenly turn in the direction of love. This change of attitude and transformation requires that an outside Power or Spirit that acts like a catalyst bring together discordant elements into a new unity.

If a person corresponds with this impulse from without, it is like turning on radio waves of speech, music, humor and learning which fill the air. But these blessings do not affect the person until he is at the proper wavelength and tunes himself in.

Sometimes our dreams reveal the religious and moral state of the subconscious mind. Carl Jung holds that every dream is a manifestation of our spiritual state; the interpretation, however, is not always easy. E.N. Ducker tells the story of a woman who came to him with a dream that an old china closet was given to her which she did not want. She took it to a dealer, convinced that it was worthless, and he paid her ten thousand dollars. He took a piece of sandpaper and rubbed off the gaudy paint, and there underneath it was gold. After she got the money, she tried to find the person who gave it to her, but he was gone. Ducker explained the dream as follows: the china closet was herself, whom she regarded as worthless, in monetary value worth only a few cents. The dealer was identified as Our Lord Who saw her real worth, that is, in terms of gold, a genuine treasure. The gaudy paint which covered the gold was her conscious approach to life. She was doing things to catch the eye, to appear significant, to impress the world and to endow herself with value. The ten thousand dollars was her true value, which the Lord put upon her. She tried to find Him again, but He was gone, with the result that she had to accept the value which the Lord had put upon her.

Jung says very often that dreams are compensations also for wrong opinions we have of ourselves. He tells of one of his patients who had an exalted opinion of himself and was unaware that everyone who knew him was irritated by his air of superiority. He came to Dr. Jung with a dream in which he had seen a drunken tramp rolling into a ditch — a sight which provoked him to say, "It is terrible to see how low a man can fall." The psychiatrist says that it was evidently a dream in part compensating for his own inflated opinion of himself, but there was something more to it than that. It turned out that he had a brother who was a degenerate alcoholic. What the dream also revealed was that his superior attitude was compensating the brother.

The world is not as irreligious as it seems at first glance. Religion has moved out of churches, to a large extent, to cope with our frustrations, despairs, shames and neuroses. The only mistake the churches can make in the new order is to assume that everybody must come to them instead of their going to everybody.

## The Closed Door

The famous painting by Holman Hunt entitled "Opportunity" pictures Christ at an ivy-clad door, knocking. Hunt has been criticized for not putting a latch on the outside of the door. The answer of the artist was, "The door is opened from the inside."

His words were a confirmation of the story of opportunity. "Behold, I stand at the door and knock. If anyone hear My Voice and open the door, I will come in to him and will dine with him and he with Me." These gracious words declare the long suffering of Our Lord as He waits for the conversion of sinners; but the love which seeks to bring that conversion about is a knock. The knock is an inspiration, a thought, an intuition — anything which seems to spring up from our subconscious mind, either telling us that we are on the wrong path or showing us the right path. It is unfortunate that we have come to think of the subconscious mind as being a kind of cesspool or garbage can, in which all the refuse of the conscious mind is thrown. Actually, the subconscious mind is the cellar door or rear entrance into the conscious mind by which Divinity gains admittance, almost surreptitiously.

It would seem that it should be man who is knocking for blessing and for pardon, but actually the situation is reversed: Divinity condescends to stand at our door and knock. The knocking is likened to those half-conscious calls which may be heard in a moment of quiet or even in times of sickness and trouble, and by which the Divine Lover makes His Presence known. But the voice is that which interprets the knock and informs us of the Personality of Him Who seeks entrance. No entry is forced; it is still within our power to disregard the knock, to ignore the Voice and to keep the door shut. The taking of food is an outward sign of brotherly love and reconciliation, for here the Tremendous Lover Who is not driven away comes in to dine with us. This represents the final stage of peace, contentment and happiness.

There is an estrangement of the human heart from God, as conscience bears witness. However much room there be for other guests in the soul, the Bethlehem story is still true: "There is no room in the inn." It is more often in souls that recognize their own misery and sinfulness that He is given room, as it was the stable rather than the inn which welcomed Him. What we call fate is actually opening the door, for He Who knocks never comes empty-handed. The unrest and discontent which dog the steps of a man who is a sinner and denies sin is but the application of the Divine Visitor's hand to the obstinately closed door. The stings of conscience, the movements of the spirit... what are these but appeals working through the subconscious mind?

The door of the soul is closed to the entrance of Truth by error, ignorance and prejudice; the door of the heart is closed by pride and unbelief and willful evil, and the door of conscience is barred by the continual habit of evil. But the knocking is repeated, and He Who stands at the door is that Love "we fall just short of in all love."

## Dialogue

The greatest untapped reservoir of energy in the universe is the depths of our own souls. Though we live with self for a lifetime, we seem to know other persons better; at any rate, we judge them more often than we do ourselves, and we analyze them better than ourselves.

An imaginary self and a real self make up the person. We strive to present the first and to neglect the second. We wear a mask whenever we go out in company. As a traitor to his country once said to his wife as they left the house for the evening, "Now, let's put on our party face." Life to a great extent becomes like a masquerade ball, in which we know that everyone is wearing a mask, and yet there is a tacit agreement that no one will tear off another's mask.

It was only natural that there should come along a philosopher to justify the mask, and that was

Sartre, who completely denied the real self or an inner life. Man to him is just as he appears on the outside. A street cleaner is a street cleaner. As he put it, "I cannot know myself except through the intermediary of another person." This means that we lack all powers of introspection; other persons are to us only mirrors reflecting back the image of self. We are stimulated and we react.

Normal persons would do well to analyze themselves and not come to know themselves only through analysis of someone else. They forget that there is such a thing as looking inward, the turning back upon oneself; this is called reflection. Often at night we see ourselves as we really are, and we shudder at the image of the true self and quickly reach, even in the dark, for our mask. Sleeping tablets numb both the burning repartee of the real self and the terrible burden of the make-believe.

It is interesting too that most of our relationships with other people are contacts, as one billiard ball contacts another billiard ball. We become like oranges in a box; we mingle with others externally, but do not commune with others in a common task. "News of the hour, on the hour" keeps us buried in the trivialities of external stimuli, lulling us into the belief that we are in contact with reality. The inner life is never given a moment to see ourselves as we really are.

How the modern world needs a Socrates, who

used to walk into the market place of Athens asking people questions in order to make them discover themselves! True, he was put to death for unmasking others, but he left the world the heritage of "know thyself."

To have the courage to look into ourselves is the beginning of a dialogue that takes place between the mask and the face, the shadow self and the real self. Once this dialogue has been achieved honestly, then there opens another dialogue — that of the soul with God. We cannot have communications with heaven until we have communications with ourselves. The prayerless people are the masked people.

When we wear the mask, we talk about the weather at cocktail parties in order that we will not have to be embarrassed by revealing our true self, but in the dialogue with self, the subject is: "How do I stand, not in the face of my fellowman, but in the face of the One Who will judge me?" This kind of conversation is not intellectual; it is rather anecdotal, as the Bible is anecdotal, as the *Iliad* and *Odyssey* are anecdotal. For here we have not a tale, but the experience of a personal truth. The soul is then no longer like the husband who keeps from his wife things that she should know as he asks, "Should I tell my wife?" Once the soul truly discovers itself, then there is nothing to be hidden either from the self or the wife or from God. It is a mark of sanity to "talk to yourself" provided the subject is the *real* self.

OUR SEARCHINGS

Many changes have taken place in the field of psychiatry in recent years. Psychiatry formerly believed that man was determined, to a great extent, by subconscious repressions; the new psychiatry is much more concerned with that which makes man human — namely, his reason — and attributes many of the ills of the mind to a want of purpose in life. It is true that a melancholy majority of men do not choose a course in life, but rather allow it to be made for them by circumstances and the outward influences of eye and ear which happen to beat upon their minds. There may be a decision to take a 7:15 a.m. train to the city, but there is a general want of an overall purpose in life. Standing at the parting of the ways, these people lack a clear notion of what they are aiming at, and allow themselves to be pressured by impulse, like weeds in a stream which move with the current or like jellyfish that are borne along by the waves. God meant that we should be hammers and not anvils. "Choose you this day whom you will serve."

What is history but the record of the tragedy of evil choice? Two alternatives are always before us. One is to work out our impulse toward truth and goodness and love of neighbor; the other is to have our lives determined from without by a rabble of confusion.

It is not enough, however, to know an ideal. One must be prepared to serve it at any cost. Principles are of little value unless we are prepared to live in accordance with them. The past is past, the future is God's, the present alone is ours. The present, however, is not a fleeting moment, but one pregnant with sacredness and infinite value. As Emerson said, "The present hour is the decisive hour, and every day is doomsday." The poet Whittier expressed it:

> *The Present, the Present is all thou hast*
> *For thy sure possessing;*
> *Like the patriarch's angel hold it fast*
> *'Til it gives its blessing.*
> *Then of what is to be, and of what is done,*
> *Why queriest thou?*
> *The past and the time to be are one,*
> *And both are Now.*

When clay is on the potter's wheel, the lightest touch of the finger can impress it with any pattern he desires; when it is taken off and hardened, nothing will change the shape of the vase except smashing it to fragments. Lord Byron, looking back on his life of wrong choices, said, "I have not had ten happy days." Lord Chesterfield declared, "I have been the whole round of pleasure, and I am disgusted." Simone de Beauvoir in her autobiography states that she has sounded all of the pleasures of life, and concludes, "I have been gypped by life."

Freedom of choice is too frequently a beautiful and dangerous gift which, like a sword in the hands of a child, injures us. But we cannot divest ourselves of our responsibility, not even by calling it a complex. Neutrality and compromise are impossible in life. If God be not the Object of adoration, then any occupant of the throne must be considered as His enemy. Dagon must fall from his pedestal when the ark of God's Presence enters the chamber of the heart. Both God and mammon cannot be served. Once religion is chosen, then it modifies the character of every action, transforming it into an offering laid upon the altar to the glory of God. All that we have and are we send to the mint and receive back stamped with the Divine Image and fashioned according to His desire.

## Wars Inside and Out

It is an illusion to believe that we should not always be without war. War is the law of life. Here we are speaking not about wars among nations, but about another kind of war, which is to be waged against evil. Even heaven itself had a battle, in which Michael flashed an archangel spear against rebels who fought not for justice, but evil. Freedom has within itself the frightening power of turning an angel into a devil.

War seems to go on even in creation, as Genesis pictures the gradual emergence of light over darkness and creation over chaos. Written across the universe is the law, "No one shall be crowned unless he has struggled." God came to this earth to reaffirm the importance of struggle. "I came not to bring peace, but the sword."

There are two kinds of swords: one that swings outward, and the other, which is thrust inward. One is to harm the neighbor, such as the sword of Peter that hacked off the ear of the high priest's servant. It was this kind of sword the Divine Master bade be put back into its scabbard. The other kind of sword is the one that cuts out egotism and selfishness and greed. The first sword, which nations hold, creates wars against others; the spiritual sword is a sign of war against ourselves. The less men wage war against the evil in their own breasts, the more they will wage war against their neighbors and nations. The more they battle against their own sins, the less need there is to do battle with the enemy without. The less we shed our own blood figuratively, the more we shed our neighbor's blood physically. Self-righteousness in persons and civil strife against neighbor go hand in hand.

He who does not find the enemy within will

find the enemy without. Every man has a civil war going on inside his own breast. If he does not bring this civil war, which is a struggle between the higher and lower self, to a victory of the spirit, he will invariably extend that civil strife to the outside. He who does not crucify his own concupiscences and his libidos will nail others to a cross. He who does not take up his own cross will lay it in contemptible self-righteousness upon the back of a neighbor.

We often wonder why there is little peace on the inside of our hearts. The real answer is that there is no peace on the inside because we are not at war with ourselves; we are not at war with ourselves because we deny that there is an enemy within to be conquered. He is never at war with himself who has never had a thought of the goodness and the holiness of God. Self-interest is his law, self-love his inspiration, self-satisfaction his end and self his god.

But look at that same man after he begins, under the inspiration of grace, to wield the sword the Master brought. Thanks to the peace that is within, his stiff, unbending self becomes supple and kind; unlovely expressions are wiped from his features. The truth has laid hold of him, has entered into him, has won his approbation, becomes his intense desire.

But...

Whenever anyone begins to compliment you in such a way as this: "You acted well, you moved about the stage gracefully, your diction was good, your character portrayal was fair" — the word you always expect next is "but." One sometimes wonders if it is not one of the most important words in our language. It always represents a hesitation, a doubt, a compromise. Christianity may be growing in the world, but if it is growing, it is growing like a goat — it has a butt.

Somewhere on a journey to Jerusalem three young men came to Our Blessed Lord. The first two said, "I will follow You," but to the third Our Lord said, "Follow Me." The first two offered their services and their submission; the third was given a summons. But in each case there was a "but." What the particular hesitations were are no different from those which postpone the peremptory decision of religion. One man might say, "Lord, I will follow You, but the nature of my business prevents me," or, "Lord, I will follow You, but there are yet a few doubts that I would like to clear up," or, "Lord, I will follow, but —

> *"First, I would see the end of this high road*
> *That stretches straight before me, fair and broad:*
> *So clear the way — I cannot go astray,*
> *It surely leads me equally to God."*

The first would-be follower was rather rash, setting no limits to his discipleship. He was ready to go anywhere, until Our Blessed Lord put before him

His own abject condition. "The foxes have holes, and the birds of the sky have nests; the Son of Man has nowhere to lay His Head." At this point the "but" came into the mind of the young man, for when he said he would follow, he never imagined that he would have to stoop to One Whose circumstances were so indigent.

The second man was willing to follow Him, but he laid down one condition: "Lord, let me first go bury my father." To him Our Lord answered, "Follow me, and let the dead bury their own dead; you, rather, go and proclaim God's Kingdom."

The third had a social but, so he asked, "Let me first take leave of my friends." To him the answer, "No one who looks behind him, when he has once put his hand to the plough, is fit for the Kingdom of God."

In each and every instance there is the rejection of conditional discipleship. The word "but" undermined the highest resolves and spoiled the fairest offers. True religion demands unconditional commitment. Augustine, before his conversion, used to say, "Dear Lord, I want to be better, but not right now — a little later on." There can be danger in delay. Julius Caesar had a letter given to him by Artemidorus the morning he went to the Senate. That letter told him about a conspiracy that was on foot to murder him, and how he might easily prevent his death; but he neglected to read it and was killed by Brutus. The answer of the Lord to the would-be followers was taken from the plowman who cannot make straight furrows if he looks back. Looking back denotes a hankering for the world, and he who looks back, later goes back. The meanest occupations demand a fixed attention and devotedness of purpose. If the plowman and the oarsman and the helmsman must have a fixed eye, then so must those who follow the Master.

## How to Become Neurotic

1. *Deny there is such a thing as guilt.* Start with the assumption that you are responsible only for the good you do, but not the wrong. Insist on praise, recognition and honor for what you consider work well done, but attribute the evil in your life to either your mother or father, your grandmother or grandfather, or because in school someone called you an idiot and your family had only a Chevrolet in a Buick neighborhood.

2. *Next, make yourself a judge of others.* Once you deny guilt and sin, then proceed to find everyone else guilty. This will take your

mind off the judgment which your conscience makes against yourself. This incessant faultfinding will release in you the
mechanism of self-justification and help
make you more "innocent" than ever. Read a
lot of gossip columns, for this will also help
to repress your real guilt by finding others
more guilty.

3. *When you are judged, immediately become
   irritated.* Let your anger increase the more
   you recognize that the criticism is justified.
   If you refuse to take the advice of your wife
   to take a particular road while motoring,
   and your decision proves to be wrong, get
   mad at her for not explaining it more
   properly.

4. *After becoming irritated against your neighbor,
   next become irritated against God.* Make fun
   of religion. Seek out its failures in certain
   individuals who professed to be religious
   and make them stand for the Church itself;
   develop a grudge against God; finally, deny
   His existence and thus make yourself a god.
   Just as you projected your guilt on your
   fellow man by hyper-criticism, so now you
   can ease your uneasy conscience by blaming
   your guilt on God.

5. *Become hard, obdurate and rebellious.* If you
   are young, begin smashing things. This will

enable you to give strength to your individual hatred of everybody and of Him Who made everybody. Your irritation thus becomes obduracy and finally aggression until you find it "hard to live with people" — they are so unappreciative of you.

6. *Go to a psychoanalyst, not a psychiatrist.* Choose particularly the psychoanalyst who will: (1) tell you that all guilt is abnormal; (2) tell you that you need more liberation through sexual license; (3) tell you that your false sense of guilt is due to an Oedipus complex if you're a man, and an Electra complex if you're a woman. Carefully avoid reading good books by such psychiatrists as Paul Tournier or anyone else who holds that abnormal manifestations of guilt have a true guilt at their base. You now will have a full-blown neurosis, which a great psychiatrist has described as "a failure to exonerate oneself from guilt."

7. *Crush immediately all promptings from God to recognize that your denial of sin is worse than your sin.* These promptings, also from the subconscious mind, are what are known as actual graces. Though they bid you see that your denial of vision makes your blindness incurable, crush them immediately. Call them crutches and say to yourself, "Why

should I lean on anyone else? I am my own creator, my own savior. My eye has its own light, my stomach has its own food, my ear needs no harmonies outside itself, my mind needs no teacher, my guilt needs no— I have no guilt." You are now fixed in your neurosis. From this point on, all you need do is find it less burdensome. Alcoholism will help until your head becomes clear, then you will have to drink again to repress the guilt; sleeping tablets will produce an unconsciousness, but you will become more uneasy when you awake. Your tolerance for human distress, poverty, dryness and infirmity will become less and less, for they are reminders that you should not spend everything on yourself. Your cynicism will make you take refuge in meaningless aphorisms about life, such as, "If you don't expect anything from life, you are never disappointed." One recalls what Simenon observed: "And if you don't breathe, you never swallow microbes."

Follow the above rules, and you will develop a neurosis made from the guiltlessness and the innocence of your sweet life and the wickedness and the brutality of the lives of others. And in the last analysis, what is your neurosis? Cowardice. The seeking for explanations instead of forgiveness. The mistaking of a cross for a crutch. What fools we mortals be. A crutch is something we lean on; a cross is something that leans on us — for healing.

## Reasons and Excuses

A reason is something we give before a conclusion is reached; an excuse is something we give for not following out the conclusion. Reasons generally are sincere; excuses generally are a rationalization of conduct. A reason is a reality; an excuse is an invention, or at least a weak reason.

The reason Adam ate the forbidden fruit was because it was sensibly pleasing to him; the excuse was that Eve gave it to him. The reason the man in the Gospel "hid his talent" was that he was indifferent and lazy, "a wicked and slothful servant." The excuse was that the master was "a hard man." The reason men did not come to the Gospel banquet was because they were all dedicated either to their possessions, to the things that made them proud, or else because they were indifferent to the Divine Food served at the banquet of Eternal Life. Their excuses were: a newly purchased field that had to be seen, five new yoke of oxen that had to be tried and a wife that had to be loved.

That is why in dealing with people it is not so important to know what people say, but rather why they say it. A writer may give very elaborate historical reasons why he hates a particular religion; but these are not nearly so important as to discover the psychological motivation for the attack. Perhaps he left that religion; perhaps he left morality. But somewhere there will be discovered the real why of the hatred. The real causes are seldom avowed, particularly in spiritual matters; these are concealed and others are suggested which serve the immediate purpose.

One day Lincoln was entering a hospital in Alexandria, Virginia. A young man running into the hospital knocked Lincoln sprawling on the sidewalk. He did not know Lincoln, but immediately began to excoriate him saying, "You big, long, lean, lanky stiff — why don't you watch where you are going?" Lincoln looked up and said, "Young man, what's troubling you on the inside?" Lincoln, with his very profound knowledge of human nature, was not so much interested in the external as he was in the warped mind and heart of the young man that had provoked his rash judgment.

A person who rightly uses his reason does so in order to take an impartial stock of the evidence and, insofar as it is possible, to keep his wishes and above all his unconscious mind out of the whole business.

Psychoanalysis does a world of good when it skims off the superficial justification for actions and discovers the real reason beneath. But there is no field in which more excuses are given than in the realm of the spiritual and the moral. Any excuse is better than none for the acceptance of the word of God, which demands the pricking of the balloon of pride, and the surrender of the illegitimate revels of the flesh. That is why there has to be a Day of Judgment to send the excuses to Hell and the reasons to Heaven.

## Why We Fail

It is not always true that "nothing succeeds like success." The lust for success may make us work so hard that we beget failure. Businessmen low down on the totem pole of a big corporation may constantly send memos to the boss to attract his attention, with the result that the boss puts them down as a bore or a pest. Golfers who are determined to be successful as long-ball hitters try so hard that they spoil their rhythm and end up as dubs. A teacher who is resolved to be a success uses such big words and amasses such confused and unrelated blobs of knowledge that the pupils cannot understand him.

I have found, after thirty years in universities, that the more books a professor brings into class, the less prepared he is. One of the greatest failures I ever knew as a teacher was one who used a cart to haul into the classroom his undigested but seeming knowledge. A speaker who yearns to be a success, cultivates poses, changes his voice and affects humor, so destroys his personality in the end that no auditor believes him to be sincere. Elderly unmarried women who want to be married try so hard to succeed that they alienate men by forward approaches which remove from men all challenge and the joy of pursuit. Anxiety about success leads to failure.

Another reason for failure is being stuck up and inflated about our own importance. Adler has called this an "inferiority complex." A more proper name would be a "superiority complex." Such people in their own estimation are not in caves, but on pinnacles. Inferiority is not a complex with the proud; it is a reflex. The egotist reacts to every situation so as to make himself the leader of the parade. A very pompous bishop was once described by a group of the junior clergy as a "one-man procession."

Because we generally bump up against people who are our superiors because they are more beautiful, better singers, etc., we become saddened; then, in our unconfessed heart of hearts, we know that we are failures. What are two ways to escape this failure completely? The first is to enter into ourselves and find out what we really are. As a business firm calls in an outside certified accountant, so we take stock of ourselves. The reason for doing this is that there are two kinds of truth in the world: outside truth and inside truth. Outside truth is what we learn in school about things and history, and read about in the daily press — truths that do not affect us any more than passing traffic. Inside truth is something that sweeps inside of us, controls us, makes us see ourselves as in a mirror; inside truth makes us look at ourselves as we do when awakening at night in the dark. Inside truth is honesty; that is why, in certain flashes of our real nature, we feel awkward, ashamed and haunted by our meanness, our brutality and our selfishness. Sometimes other people get inside us and we react, "That person gets on my nerves." It is when we reach the point where we say that of ourselves that we have the true estimate of our worth.

Once conscious of our capital and real worth, we can now go forth to meet new challenges; maybe learn a new language, take up painting or, better still, begin to serve our neighbors. Knowing our limitations in one direction, we are better prepared to develop the talents we have in the right direction.

The second therapeutic for our vaulting pride is reliance and trust in God. There are here two extremes to be avoided: one is to believe that man does everything and God does nothing, which is the

Western sin of pride; the other is to believe that God does everything and man does nothing, which is the Oriental sin of fatalism. The golden truth is between the two, as expressed by Paul: "I can do all things in Him Who strengthens me." One then discovers inner peace, which comes from doing the best one can while relying on God's help. If there is success, there is a thanksgiving; if there is no success, then one still accepts the Divine Purpose.

In the Divine Order, what generally seems at first a failure may be a vestibule for a further success. St. Paul was told if he went to Jerusalem, he would be bound and imprisoned. Paul went anyway, knowing it was his duty. He was cast into jail and the Word of the Lord came to him. "Take courage, as you have testified about Me in Jerusalem, so you shall bear witness to Me in Rome."

What was a failure was turned into a tremendous success in a new missionary endeavor. Sometimes nothing succeeds like failure.

## Who Not to Consult

In a world in which minds are bewildered by problems of life, marriage, ethics in business and medicine, broken homes and shattered hearts, to whom should one turn for direction?

In general there are three types one should generally avoid, though there are particular circumstances in which consultation might be profitable. It is obvious that here we are referring not to problems of the mechanical, economic, legal or international order, but rather to those which are moral, spiritual and ethical.

In general, one should not consult the young. Not only are they lacking in experience, but there is also the possibility that they may "throw the book" at the person in trouble. They have not lived long enough to be able to make a transfer from the abstract knowledge they have of a problem to the very concrete case before them.

Knowledge is like timber: it is better when aged. In the scientific or political order, however, youth often surpasses maturity. At the age of twenty-seven, Napoleon executed his great military campaign in Italy and drove back the routed Austrians to their capital. The King of Babylon chose young men, well-favored, without blemish and with great ability to stand before him. But the moral leadership of the young did not equal their political acumen.

Every adolescent is an adverb turning into a personal pronoun of either he or she. Until that maturity is reached, it is not well to seek moral guidance from youth, unless they are saints in the making.

It will be recalled that the young men counseled King Rehoboam to be cruel, a policy which proved to be wrong. Sometimes the self-will of youth makes it impossible for them to enter into the will of others. Our Blessed Lord told Peter how differently he would act when he was old than when he was young. "When you were young you fastened your belt and went where you wanted, but when you're old you'll stretch out your hands and another will fasten you and bring you where you don't wish to go."

The second type of counselor that should be avoided is the one who is immoral. An adulterer should not be consulted about purity, a thief about honesty, a divorced man about the meaning of marriage, a careless parent about juvenile delinquency or a crooked politician about international rights. Before seeking the guidance of a legislator about a minimum wage law, it is always well to find out how much he pays his servants. The robber does not want to have a policeman's light shining upon him as he robs a safe. Neither do the evil like to have the moral law shining upon them in their misdeeds. In their darkness they are incapable of taking a bewildered hand in the shadow and leading it into the light.

How very different is teaching from counseling. An immoral man is just as capable of teaching higher mathematics as a moral man. In fact, if his intellectual preparation and equipment are better, his teaching is more perfect. But when one comes to what is called the practical intellect, as distinguished from the speculative, then the way a person lives determines the way he thinks. If a husband or wife, therefore, are having marital troubles, it would always be well to find out from the marriage counselor or psychiatrist, before they consult him, if the man beats his wife.

A third type of counselor to be avoided is one who is always active, but never contemplative. He who is caught up in the whirlpool of life can never extricate another from its whirling waters. Martha, who was busy about many things, was not as good at advising others as Mary, who sat at the feet of the Master in quiet and contemplation. One of the wisest of sayings is that of one of the most learned men who ever lived, Thomas Aquinas: *"Contemplata aliis tradere"* — "We deliver to others those things upon which we have meditated."

## Whom to Consult

We spoke of three kinds of counselors to avoid if one seeks advice in the spiritual or moral order. We come now to the positive side of counseling. The best one to consult is one who has suffered. Here we do not mean suffering only from a physical point of view, but rather one who has suffered with meaning, seeing in it a kind of Good Friday that leads to an Easter Sunday; one who sees suffering as a fire that purges away dross to make the gold finer; one who envisages pain as a kind of a detachment from the material that makes attachment to the spiritual easier. This kind of suffering always makes it possible to identify oneself with the other. The suffering may be physical, mental, social or moral, and from it comes not learning, but wisdom. In *The Teahouse of the August Moon* the wisdom of Sakini is given: "Pain makes men think; thought makes men wise; wisdom makes life endurable."

Pius XII, just a short time before he died, told someone whom I know very well, "You have suffered a great deal and it has been difficult." The speaker said to him, "But I would not be without it, for it has drawn me closer to God." Pius XII answered, "That is right. We get learning from books, but we get wisdom from suffering."

When Moses was on the mountaintop, the Lord said to him, "I am coming to you in a dense cloud, so that when the people hear Me speaking with you, they may always have faith in you also and obey you without question henceforward." God wished to make a man to speak to people; should He leave his energies unimpaired for the great work that he is to do? Rather, because Moses was destined to be the great counselor of people, God fitted him for the task by making him pass through a dark cloud. Far from hiding God, the cloud brings Him to the soul. It was here that Moses derived his eloquence as a speaker, his force as a teacher and his inspiration as a counselor.

No man can ever impress another man and lead him out of the depths unless he himself has met God in a dark cloud. It is not enough that one should merely speak to God; he must see Him in a storm. Men who live in gardens amid fruits and flowers and bask in perpetual sunshine can give counsel when money is in the bank, when the blood tingles in the veins and when the heart is light. But when woes, worries, wounds and distress come, then only the man who has lived in the shadow of the cross can advise. Only a man with scars can help the wounded; only one who has stumbled to his throne can lift up the fallen; only the afflicted can bring comfort to those in affliction; that is why only a God Who has come to this world and taken up a cross can ever give the final consolation. "It is not as if our High Priest was incapable of feeling for us in our humiliations; He has been through every trial, fashioned as we are, only sinless."

## Leisure

Leisure is taken from the Greek word *skole*, from which our word school is derived. School, therefore, was a place of leisure, inasmuch as it enabled one to perfect his mind by a kind of contemplation. The Latins had the word *neg-otium*, which is the negation of leisure or ease and, therefore, means business. The use of the English word negotiations for business is an apt description of the very denial of leisure which is so necessary for the human mind.

Leisure, therefore, is not idleness or incapacity, but a spiritual and moral quality of the soul. It has nothing to do with external factors, for example, a day off from work, a holiday, a weekend vacation, a day at the golf course. Pieper, in analyzing leisure, has given the following factors:

Leisure is a form of silence, not noiselessness. It is the silence of contemplation such as occurs when we let our minds rest on a rosebud, a child at play, a Divine mystery or a waterfall. As the Book of Job puts it, "God gives songs in the night."

Silence is something like that wordlessness which happens between lovers. As Maeterlinck said, "It is only before strangers that we must speak."

True leisure is not an interruption from work, a coffee break, a recess. It is not at all in the same line as work, but rather passes at right angles to it. It is not a pick-me-up for work. It is not something for "iron-poor blood." Leisure is the capacity to raise the heart and mind out of the workaday world, to get in touch with superhuman lifegiving powers. It is a recognition that "every man has a hole in his head" into which, as William James has said, "saving influences pour."

Labor Day is a relic of the time when men worshiped on feast days and holy days. When God rested on the seventh day, He made that the day of worship.

Throughout history there was land that was set apart for a temple, and that land was regarded as holy; so too, there was a time separated from work which also became related to the temple, or worship. Hence, the seventh day was a day of rest and worship. As worship passes out of life, leisure becomes impossible. It reduces itself either to laziness or boredom, emptiness or compulsion. As Baudelaire wrote, "One must work, if not from taste, then at least from despair." Work is accepted because it is less boring than pleasure.

Socialism emphasizes "the worker" and not the person. Such is one of the effects of the denial of leisure for the mind and worship, and to remind us that the whole of our being is not satisfied with six days of profit-making. Where there is culture, there is leisure; and where there is leisure, there is worship.

As Dostoevski has said, "A man who bows down to nothing can never bear the burden of himself."

## The Quiet Time

Hippocrates, the ancient Greek physician who inspired the Hippocratic oath which all doctors take, wrote, "I shall keep my life pure and undefiled, and my art also." This doctor also wrote a line which has struck modern medicine and psychiatrists profoundly: "Meditation is for a man's spirit what walking is for his body."

The word meditation is rather an abused word, for it conjures up certain formulas of prayer, such as the Ignatian method and the Salesian method, which so formalize thinking as to destroy it. It would be much better to use the words "quiet time," in which a person shuts out the noise of the world, enters into himself and judges himself not by his press clippings, but how he stands with God. There is an old story of a Saracen woman who came to England seeking her lover. She passed through the foreign cities with no word upon her tongue that could be understood by those who heard her except the name of him whom she was seeking. Many today are wandering through the earth as strangers in the midst of it. They cannot translate the cry of their own hearts, but it really means "my soul thirsts for You." There is only One Who can respond to these deepest aspirations of the heart.

In this quiet time, we see that every single life is a summons of His voice: our sorrows by their bitterness and our joys by their quick passing alike call the heart of Him in Whom alone sorrows can be soothed and joys made full and permanent.

Each person decides for himself what is the best quiet time in his life. Some are owls, others are roosters; some are winders, others are unwinders; some are brightest and most penetrating early in the morning, others are most alert at night. This quiet time is no mere vacuum, but it is rather the door which closes on the noisy life within. As the Psalmist puts it, "Be still, and know that I am God." The quiet time is also a kind of natural fortress where one takes refuge from the emptiness and distractions and fulfills the injunction: "When you pray, go into the inner chamber and, having shut the door, pray to the Father in secret."

God does not save by the barrel load. He summons all because He summons each. He does not cast out His illuminations at random over the heads of a crowd, as a rich man might fling coins to a mob, but He addresses every one singly as if there were no other soul in the universe to hear His voice.

The quiet time individualizes this summons, appropriates it and allows us to see ourselves as we really are.

This quiet time should be a minimum of half an hour and, if possible, an hour. It takes almost a quarter of an hour to shut out the distractions of the world. One begins with a confrontation of self, denudes his pretenses, throws off the mask he wears before others and looks his faults in the face. Then there takes place an expansion of the field of consciousness which Janet tried to establish by hypnosis and Freud by the analysis of dreams and bungled action. One enters first into a dark room where there is nothing but a shapeless mass of particular problems, confused ideals and bitter remorse. Then the field of consciousness begins to contract, and one discovers in the unconsciousness what we have been hiding from ourselves. It has well been said that the practice of the quiet time leads to "a progressive recession of the frontier between the conscious and the unconscious."

Then there begins to be an encounter with Divinity, a half articulate plea for pardon and a growing assurance that heart-seeking is sure to issue in heart-finding. "Ask and you shall receive, seek and you shall find." This quiet time is an absolute necessity of life; without it, personality dies. The traveler on a journey looks forward to a spot where he can stay a while; the sailor has his haven where he can furl his sails and find shelter from the storm and tempest. The soul needs actually more rest than the body, and it could very well be that our restless soul is at the basis of many of our physical ills.

## The Secret of Meditation

"Do not walk on the thin ice," every mother tells a child who lives near a body of frozen water. Such knowledge remains a theoretical warning until the child is actually confronted with thin ice. Then the warning of the mother becomes emotionally stirred up in the mind of the child and relevant to the situation at hand. When one adds together the advice of mothers and fathers to children, the counsels of teachers, psychiatrists and preaching from the pulpit, one wonders how much good is really being done. Does not preaching refer to an object outside of the hearer? Is not its truth a kind of "it" unrelated to the "me," much as the stone a geologist picks up does not affect his own personal life?

Much of the criticism directed against religious and moral counseling is based on its inability to have concreteness, like the mother's injunction to the little girl when she got near the ice. Many of the thinkers and poets of our day believe that the solution is for man to refer all of his moods to himself, to ignore anything objective and to treat his subjective states as antennae which contact the depths within, but without a standard outside self.

While there is indeed a failure in counseling to make truth and morality personal, the answer is still not to be found simply by referring to oneself. As Kierkegaard has said, it is as if a man had been shipwrecked at a point in the sea where 70,000 fathoms of water were his whole support. A man thrown into the sea can just thrash about, without any hope of finding something substantial on which to rest.

Though many of our contemporary writers are correct in protesting against the mere indoctrination of truth which is never lived out, they have generally failed to offer the one means most calculated to make knowledge relevant and personal, and that is by meditation. Meditation acts on a person some what the same as functional medicine. Not long ago, doctors were so specialized that they treated only diseases and not sick people. Now medical practitioners affirm the necessity of treating the whole person. In like manner, it is only by meditation that one personalizes a truth.

Taking an example from Buddhism: A student is supposed to so meditate on the bull's-eye he will shoot with arrows that, after many hours of practice and meditation, he can not only hit the target with his eyes closed, but he can also make a second arrow hit the first arrow which hit the center of the target. The concentration of the student is on the *target*, and not just on the bow and arrow.

Meditation generally is considered as a reflection on something that one seizes and makes part of oneself, for example, the compassion of Our Lord in feeding the hungry multitude. Meditation, rather, is not merely thinking of compassion outside of oneself, but also trying to think oneself into compassion and mercy and kindness. Here one touches on the great difference between German and Oriental mystics on the one hand, and the great Spanish mystics on the other. The former were satisfied to be absorbed into Divinity, but the Spanish mystics, among whom the greatest was St. Teresa, tended to absorb Deity into themselves. St. Teresa wrote:

> *This Divine union of love in which I live*
> *Makes God my captive and my heart free.*
> *But it causes me such pain to see God my prisoner*
> *That I die of longing to die.*

Here there is a flaming dart plunged into the saint's passionate breast through her meditation.

One may give a thousand lectures on the chemical composition of water to a swimmer, but there is nothing like his plunging into the Mediterranean and feeling the warm water buoy him up and quicken his spirit.

How different our lives would become if we would take an hour a day not to think about the attributes of God and the moral law, but to make the love of God and the love of neighbor experientially present in our own heart and soul! Man does not want to be with God as much as God wants to be with man. This is the secret of meditation. Try it and be happy.

## *"Aye" or "Nay" to Eternal Destiny*

Often those who complain that they receive "no breaks" in life are the very ones who have not utilized their gifts. It is true that there is a diversity of talents, some being given ten, others five, and others only one; but condemnation in the Gospel is meted out only to him who does not make returns on his gift. This is because we are not merely receptive beings; we are also active. A lake, unless the living waters flow through it, becomes stagnant and putrid like the Dead Sea. The sun shines to light a world. The fleeting streams flow self-content by seeking out the ocean. The tree yields its fruit, the air ministers to life by passing through the lungs. Nature knows no arresting hand, no selfhood.

Gifts can be perverted and turned to disloyal

uses, but they can also be neglected through personal ease and indulgence. Those who have not received many gifts sometimes undervalue them with perilous modesty, forgetting that the weakest vessel can hold some water, the simplest speech can praise the Lord, a stupid ass carried Him into Jerusalem.

The muscle that is not used atrophies. The U.N. reports an increase of certain diseases in the underprivileged nations because of malnutrition. But what of the privileged nations? Among these, there is an increase of coronary thrombosis, which is attributed in part to excessive fat and want of exercise. Minds are underdeveloped because they will not put forth the energy necessary to bring them to the joy and thrill of knowledge.

In the Gospel, he who is perpetually condemned is the one who does nothing with his gifts. It was so in the case of the priest and the Levite who passed by the wounded man on the road from Jerusalem to Jericho; it was so of the rich man, of whom no ill is recorded except that a beggar lay at his gate full of sores, and yet no man gave him to eat; it was true of the servant who hid in a napkin the talent committed to him, and also of the unprofitable servant who had only done what it was his duty to do. A man plants a tree in order that it might bring forth fruit. The tree in the Gospel which bore no fruit was ordered cut down because it only cumbered the ground. God expects returns for His great and wonderful investments in us. The condemned man is the negative man who gives way to the inertia of the moment, follows the line of least resistance, remains stunted, starved and profitless to society.

The law of nature and of grace is inexorable in this matter of neglect. He who has the capacity to learn and wastes his time on mental pastry eventually reaches a point where he cannot read a good book or absorb a spiritual inspiration — not because it lacks interest but because it cannot interest him. Men may sin away the very capacity even to desire the thing they need; they can even atrophy the ability to pray. Macbeth knew what he should pray for; words were not wanting, thoughts were not wanting, but in his soul he knew that he did not wish for the very thing he ought to pray for, because he had killed the power of a better affection and aspiration.

The most serious neglect is that of soul-making. For each minute of time is given to man to say "Aye" or "Nay" to his eternal destiny. Every now and then, there bursts in upon the mind a brief light from another world, revealing the precipice that stands before one, as well as the pull of the stars. Sometimes it is darkness that gives vision scope, but even to the most neglecting souls there comes that still, quiet voice of conscience beckoning one on to peace. It is an unsolicited favor and one procured at an infinite price, but it offers deliverance, peace to men of business fretted with anxiety, to women with the care and delight of children, to youth in the full bloom and blossom of springtime promise, to the aged that the greatest life is yet beyond. This is a special kind of peace; it is above the human; it is also free. That is why it is called "grace." For a people to be living in a plague and refuse the antidote which could cure would be foolish. But how often it is true: "I would, but you would not." The greatest things in life are free, and greatest among these is Divine Life — if we do but seek it.

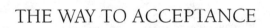

# THE WAY TO ACCEPTANCE

## Adventure

When a heart ceases to have a deep love for anything, it becomes bored. Putting the same kind of nut on the same kind of bolt day after day, hammering out meaningless correspondence on a machine, and collecting luncheon checks at a counter may all be necessary for economic livelihood, but their meaningless routine wears away and corrodes the dignity of one's personality. No wonder boys love Robinson Crusoe, teenagers love speed, businessmen want to make more money, jaded married women devour novels about romantic heroes, punk rockers thrill to snapping their fingers, flaunting their dirty clothes and shaking their long hair at the convention of their elders. They are all seeking to break out of the prison bars of the tedium of society and organization by some kind of adventure or daring. Every single person in the world has a need of fulfillment, a thirst for the absolute.

Other nations are wrong in saying that Americans are money mad. Is it money that businessmen are after, or a mysterious something which they lack? Is their drive really any different from the scientist's compulsion to do research, or the skindiver's plunge into new, unexplored depths? What really makes America great is not its wealth or its science, or its sense of mission to the rest of the world; underneath all of these is its passion for adventure, the quest of the new, whether it be a new frontier or a new combination of chemicals.

There are two kinds of adventures: *quality* adventures and *quantity* adventures. Quantity adventures are ones such as increasing one's stock holdings, escalating one's position from elevator operator to elevator starter, collecting seashells, moving from lieutenant governor to governor for the sake of power, increasing one's drug or alcohol intake or betting more often on the daily double. This kind of adventure may give excitement, but it never fulfills one's personality because there is nothing to these experiences but the addition of zeros. They are like adding boxcar to boxcar on a siding, but without an engine or a destination. To move up from a sports car to a Cadillac and then to a Rolls-Royce only means that one exchanges one dissatisfaction for another. Furthermore, all of the pleasure is outside one's personality and not inside it. Take things away and the heart is empty.

Quality adventure, on the other hand, has something to do with inner values, a drive for perfection and a quest for peace of soul. The adventure lies not in things outside the heart and mind, but within them. Among quality adventures the three most satisfying adventures are: knowledge, social service and religion.

Knowledge embraces all subjects which perfect the mind, such as empirical sciences like bio-chemistry, and the whole gamut of university studies including philosophy itself. The wise Greek, Aristotle, held that the knowledge of philosophy adds to one's existence by transmuting concrete existences into mental existence, thus enriching the joy of living. But the endless repetition of the same kind of knowledge that one finds in many a classroom is not very adventurous. Some professors are merely textbooks wired for sound. Teaching is too often reduced to the communication of the notes in the professor's yellow pages to the white pages of a student's notebook, without passing through the minds of either. Knowledge is adventurous only when it is progressive, when it tears aside old veils and reveals new horizons. One of the purest natural joys of living is the growth in the acquisition of truth.

Social service is another form of adventure and here is understood not just as sociological research into the fighting habits of racial groups, but rather as service to the world, particularly the impoverished half who go to bed hungry every night. The Peace Corps, which is the governmental side of missionary activity, is one such elevating experience. Missionaries in particular represent a special breed of the adventurous. They leave their country for life as did Abraham; they identify themselves with the people they serve; and they so love them that when they return temporarily to an affluent civilization, they are unhappy and anxious to get back to service. This kind of adventure, which identifies itself with the stricken, the hungry and the unlettered, pays the highest inner dividends, namely, the joy which comes from spending oneself and being spent in love of neighbor.

The supreme adventure is religion. By religion is not meant the sterile sitting in comfortable pews, but the response to the promise of the God-man: "I have come that you may have life and have it more abundantly." That is the point — "more abundantly." It challenges us to liquidate our unruly wills, our egocentrisms, our petty search for aloneness, and our selling a field to buy the pearl of great price. This adventure loves not the spark but the Flame. It reaches its psychological peak when it can say with Catherine of Genoa, "My 'me' is God, nor do I know my selfhood save in Him." That kind of love summons us to interest ourselves in the world, because God loves it, because God created it and is Himself engaged in this adventure. The joy of this commitment refuses to be satisfied with anything less than the totally satisfying. The totally satisfying is not something which *should* satisfy us, but something which *does* satisfy, down to the very toes of our soul.

## *The Joy of Being a Prodigal Son*

"I had a nervous breakdown" — no one ever blushes about making such a confession, even though it may have been caused by guilt. Such was the case of one whom we shall call Gerald, who had wasted away to skin and bones. He had been under psychiatric treatment for three years and had shown some slight improvement. The psychiatrist sent him to me saying, "His nervous breakdown has something behind it which I cannot find. I think it belongs in the moral order, but he is reluctant to tell me because he knows that I am not the best representative in the world of that order."

I asked Gerald a number of questions and then quickly shot in the query, "How much money did you steal?" He denied for five minutes that he had stolen anything. Repeatedly asking the question broke him down and he answered, "Three thousand dollars. But how did you know?" I told him that the description he gave of his conduct in one respect, such as wiping off money before he gave it away, gave me the suspicion that he was involved with "dirty money." Later on, he made restitution and found peace with God and, therefore, with himself.

In this world, where there is so much cheating, dishonesty and stealing, it is well to recall the stern, pedestrian fact of restitution. There are some who injure others and never ask for forgiveness; others who say they are sorry, but never mean it, like Pharaoh, whose mock repentance only hardened his soul; still others admit a fault, but, like Saul, make so many excuses that their confession only works toward despair, madness and suicide.

There are three steps in soul purgation without which true inner peace is impossible. The first is the acknowledgment of our responsibility for any moral fact, such as injuring another's reputation, adultery, theft or any such disorder. It is a humiliating step indeed to say, "I have sinned." This admission may come on one in a flash as with David, or after many sleepless nights, as with Augustine. One wonders if, in the whole of literature, there is any book which has so much contributed to the unmasking of faults as the *Confessions of St. Augustine*; few works have so prompted others to say, "It is wrong to live for myself; it is not the design of happiness. In all my pleasures I merely multiplied zeros, and now at the end have nothing but regrets."

The second point is that the guilt must be seen ultimately not as the breaking of a law, but as the wounding of Divine Love. This point of view becomes more poignant in Christianity, where every sin is seen in relation to the Crucifix. I can see the relation between any pride and the crown of thorns; my lust and the flesh hanging from His Body like purple rags; my grasping embrace of mammon or wealth in the pierced hands; my lost and errant ways in the riveted feet; and above all, my false loves in the pierced heart. Few are sorry because they broke a law; but everyone is contrite in seeing what egotism did to the Beloved. No abstractions — such as humanity or class or party — can bind a man's hot passions from their self-indulgence, or bend his proud head in penitent confession of guilt. The honest cry is the one David wrote after his adultery with Bathsheba: "Against You only have I sinned and done what is evil in Your sight."

At the root of every deed which breaks the heart and starts a civil war in the soul is the affirmation: "I am god; I am my own creator, my own redeemer." Generally, egotists are not as willing to declare their belief in this kind of god as they are to negate a belief in the God Who stirs their conscience to return to Him. Atheism is never an intellectual position, and neither is doubt or agnosticism; they are moral positions begotten of one of three kinds of behavior: pride, which refuses to bend the ego; lust or impurity, which detaches the flesh from true love; and greed or worldliness, which adds barns to barns as a kind of economic immortality.

Finally there is the pardon which comes with restitution if necessary. Pardon is not related to time. As the laws of chemistry and physics at work for years in a hidden way prepare for the "sudden" eruption of a volcano, so reconciliation with God takes place in a "sudden" moment, having been prepared for by years of concealed guilt. Alp piled upon Alp pass away as their mountainous guilts are cast into the depths of the sea. Really, the pity of life is not what men do; it is what they miss — the joy of being a prodigal son.

## Acceptance of Truth

An age of unbelief is always an age of superstition. As faith declines, credulity increases. In order to understand this statement, one must grasp the true meaning of faith. Faith today is identified with a kind of feeling or instinctive urge toward the acceptance of an idea. Very few today realize that reason is a prelude to faith. Whether they know it or not, they follow the philosophy of Jean Jacques Rousseau, who wrote to Dom Deschamps in 1762, "Order and method are your gods; they are my furies. The state of reflection is contrary to nature. A man who meditates is a depraved animal. Don't think, it hurts; just feel."

In German, Goethe made Faust say, "Feeling is everything." Madame de Stael wrote a work on the influence of passions on happiness. Wordsworth said: "Our meddling intellect misshapes the beauteous form of things."

It is very hard to convince those whose lives are dominated by feeling that faith has nothing whatever to do with emotion. Nor does it have anything to do with "feeling good," because very often faith recommends something that is very difficult, such as taking up a cross. Nor is faith something so compelling as to completely destroy reason, as if one might say, "It bowled me over."

Reason is absolutely essential as a condition of faith, for reason alone gives motives of credibility. Suppose you receive from a police station a telephone call saying your car has been stolen. It would do no good to say, "Well, I have faith that it has not," because all of the evidence is the other way. If faith be likened to the flat roof of the house, reason may be compared to the ladder. One must use the ladder to get on the roof. Once one is there, one could, if one so desired, kick away the ladder, though it would not be the proper thing to do because one must always use reason to elaborate on the faith that has been received.

It is reason that creates motives for believing. Faith is to religion very much as credit is to business. Just as one must have a reason for giving credit, so too must one have a reason for believing. The conclusions of reason for accepting the testimony of anyone — for example, the testimony of Christ — are not mathematically certain. They are only morally certain. They are very much like the certitude that you have that you were born of your own parents. If you were immediately challenged to prove that particular fact, you might be at a great loss to do so; but your certitude is greater than your reasons for your certitude. It is merely sufficient that reason be an adequate basis for a decision. Though Lord Nelson once put a telescope to his blind eye, there was still reason for believing that a telescope has the power, if applied to a seeing eye, to embrace objects which the natural eye could not see.

How does a man come to faith in the Divinity of Christ? His reason establishes certain motives of credibility, namely, (1) Anyone who comes from God should be pre-announced; (2) He should be able to work wonders and signs as an attestation that He is a Divine messenger; (3) nothing that He teaches should be contrary to human reason. Once one has the moral certitude for assenting to belief in the Divinity of Christ, then follows the act of love.

The human heart cannot love without the unseen, the invisible, the mysterious. Children must have their angels, their saints, and when they lose these, they have left only space cadets. Adults, when they lose faith, must have detective stories; as they lose the mysteries of religion, they begin to be interested in who killed the barmaid. Love has to thrive on an ideal, something unexplored. So religion is based on an eruption from an unseen order, a self-disclosure, something that is given.

When we try to make everything clear, we make everything confused. If, however, we admit one mysterious thing in the universe, then everything else becomes clear in the light of that. The sun is so bright, so mysterious, that one cannot look at it, and yet in the light of the sun everything else is seen. Chesterton said, "We can see the moon and we can see things under the moon, but the moon is the mother of lunatics."

## Faith

What is Faith? Some conceive it as believing that something will happen, such as "I have faith that I will make a fortune before I am forty." Others think of it as self-confidence and self-assurance by which they make God a junior partner in some project of theirs. "I have faith that I will woo and win that rich girl." This is not faith but egotism; it is directed not to God but to self.

Faith is related not to self-assurance but to God; not to an event, but to truth. In fact, there is often the greatest faith when there is the least prosperity. Such was the case with Job who, full of sores and sitting on a dunghill, said, "I will trust Him though He slay me." Faith is the acceptance of a truth on the authority of God revealing it. When a distinguished scientist tells me about the age of fossils, I accept it on natural faith. I never made a test of the bones to verify his estimate. But I have a sufficient motive in his credibility, namely, he is the kind of man who would neither deceive nor be deceived. Therefore his utterance about the fossil age I accept as true.

Now, over and above the human, there is the Divine. As a scientist can reveal to me truths which are beyond my reason, so God can reveal to me truths beyond the power of my intelligence. Since I know Him to be One Who neither deceives nor can be deceived, I accept His revelation in faith.

How do men receive a scientific truth which is beyond their knowledge? Some deny it, some ridicule it, some are silent through indecision. The same reactions happen in the face of a Divine Revelation. Remember the time when Our Blessed Lord cured the man who was blind from birth? The miracle was worked to prove that He was the Son of God. The miracle was to be a motive for believing in Him, just as our associations with certain people give us an assurance of their trustworthiness. But some, refusing to recognize the miracle, denied that it was the same man who was born blind: "He looks like him." In other words, "There is a fraud." But the man born blind, now restored to vision, said, "I am he."

Now that fraud had been eliminated, some

inquirers asked how the change came to pass. When he answered that the Lord did it, the answer of those who saw the miracle was, "How can a man who is a sinner do such miracles?" Here is a new escape from belief. This time, deceit is no longer the excuse from assenting to belief, but rather an attack upon character. There was a latent consciousness that "this Man performs many miracles," but they refused to draw the proper inference. The parents of the man were insulted; they verified the blindness of their son from birth, but no amount of proof could convince those who refused to be convinced. Poor mortals! So often on hearing a truth, or discovering a fact which runs counter to their prejudices, they seek to disparage it. The man who was blind could not convince them though he said, "It's unheard of that anyone ever opened the eyes of one born blind. If He were not from God, He would not be able to do anything."

In answer, those who refused to accept this conclusion attributed an evil life to the one cured. He must be rotten, a liar, a thief, an adulterer, an idiot, otherwise he would not be so believing. Later on, when Christ saw the man, He asked him, "Do you believe in the Son of God Who is speaking with you now?" He answered, "I do believe, Lord," and worshiped Him.

Faith, it will be seen, has nothing to do with expectancy, with prosperity, with fate; it is not even related to an abstract statement. It centers in a Person — a Person Who is Truth itself. It becomes a dialogue between the human and the Divine, between a dark mind and a Light, between a weak will and a surrender, between Someone toward Whom we have a motive for believing and our poor self who eats the offered bread, though we know not all the mysteries of physiological digestion. Without that Someone, we all have an enfeebling sense of blindness; but when His Truth is accepted, we no longer stumble, but walk, yes, run into the Ineffable Light of the Perfect Day.

## Health and Holiness

The accumulated wisdom of the human race has always acknowledged that there was some kind of relationship between peace of soul and health. "A healthy mind in a healthy body" is only an abbreviation of a statement from the Latin poet Juvenal, who wrote in his satires, "Your prayer must be that you may have a sound mind in a sound body." A more modern poet, Francis Thompson, wrote, "Holiness is an oil which increases a hundredfold the energies of the body, which is the wick." The Austrians had a proverb: "A sad saint is a sorry sort of a saint."

Today, however, medicine and psychiatry are combining to prove that there is some intrinsic relationship between holiness and health. The French tradition of medicine has always believed in a long interrogation of the patient in order to view the drama of his human life. A treatise by the well-known Swiss psychiatrist Dr. Paul Tournier, entitled *The Healing of Persons*, is a wonderful contribution to a synthesis of modern psychology and the Christian faith. He holds that the physical problems of a person's life often correspond to mental problems and both of these, in turn, to spiritual problems. There is no physical reform possible without a moral reform. And there is no moral reform without a spiritual renewal. This boils down to saying that behavior and a mode of life are very important factors in determining health. Symptoms, he holds, may be exaggerated forms of normal defense reactions; they are abnormal as far as disease is concerned, but they may be normal as far as the defensive reaction is concerned.

A confirmation of this idea comes from Dr. Swain of Boston, who wrote of 270 cases in which the patient was cured on being freed from fear, worry and resentment. His conclusion was that sixty per cent of arthritis cases had their origin in moral conflict. Everyone is familiar with the conclusions of Dr. Karl A. Menninger, who stresses the influence of the state of mind on the condition of those suffering from high blood pressure. The latter often seems to be a sort of physical expression of a moral hypertension which paralyzes it. Dr. Alexis Carrel, speaking of the alarming increase of neurosis and psychosis over the last hundred years, states that this increase "can be more dangerous for civilization than infectious diseases. Mental diseases by themselves are more numerous than all other diseases put together." Dr. Tournier holds that "all functional disturbances and, *a fortiori*, all neuroses, may be seen to involve thus a secret flight into disease. This, of course, is not to say that the disease itself is imaginary.... How many women there are who have a migraine every time they receive an invitation to visit their hostile in-laws."

Some years ago, Dr. C.G. Jung made a statement which has been quoted many times: "During the past thirty years, people from all civilized countries of the earth have consulted me.... Among all my patients in the second half of life — that is to say, over thirty-five — there has not been one whose problem in the last resort was not that of finding a religious outlook on life. It is safe to say that every one of them fell ill because he had lost that which the living religions of every age have given to their followers, and none of them had really been healed who did not regain his religious outlook."

The vocation of a doctor may have been very much underrated. His ideal is not just to cure a patient of neuralgia or phobias, but also to be at one and the same time an educator, a politician, a man of God, a philosopher and a theologian, not in the sense that he takes over completely any of these functions, but rather that he recognizes that every sick person in the world has, to some extent, a combination of three disorders: physical, psychic and spiritual.

## The Last Night

Christian truths, when they are rejected and denied, have a way of coming back like ghosts to haunt us. Take for example the notion of hell. After having denied it on the outside, hell moved to the inside, as modern man battles with the specters and ghosts and devils in his subconscious mind.

Another item in the creed which we believed we had intellectually surpassed was the end of the world and the last judgment. Today no talk is more common than the end of the world and the judgment of a nuclear war. The scriptural idea of a violent, catastrophic and sudden end of the world like the flash of lightning from the east to the west was scrapped; it was thought to be unbecoming to the evolutionary concept of unlimited progress. In this hour, the language of that horrible end is back again as man shrinks in fear, not from the judgment of God, but from the judgment of man. We now sit as startled beings waiting for the dread hour when, as it were, someone would throw a brick into the city's dynamo and all the lights would go out; or else when some human demon would poison the reservoirs of the world and we would perish in thirst.

The late C.S. Lewis, professor of literature at Oxford, has given to the catastrophic ending of the earth the title which he took from John Donne: "The World's Last Night." He stresses not so much the bomb shelter which will protect from the burning of a fissioned atom, but rather that clarity of conscience which alone is the safeguard in that apocalyptic night. As he puts it, "The schoolboy does not know which part of his Virgil lesson he will be made to translate; that is why he must be prepared to translate any passage. The sentry does not know at what time an enemy will attack or an officer will inspect his post; that is why he must keep awake all the time."

Thus those who denied that the Great Dramatist would have a last curtain now, as spectators, dread not the Dramatist, but that they may pull the curtain of doom upon themselves. When King David was asked whether he would prefer to be judged by men or by God, he chose the judgment of God, for the latter would be more tolerable. Our century, without such a conscious choice, is living in fear of what man, in a foolish moment, may do to the world.

The point of it all is not to increase fear and drive men, like groundhogs, into hysteria away from the Light. Perhaps the lesson of the fright of the world's last night is that what we should be doing is this: going through our wastebaskets to pick out the great discarded spiritual and moral truths that we have been casting into it for the last few centuries.

## The Great Heart of God

Goethe wrote that everyone brings fear into the world, but not reverence. A bad conscience keeps a lot of snakes coiled within itself, and at night the nocturnal brood come out with their bitter fangs of poisonous remorse. But because men cannot quiet their hearts by themselves, it is not therefore true that the heart cannot find peace.

There may be times when our heart chides us that we have fallen far below our ideals, but with amendment one can always be sure of the Father's Love. There are always sensitive souls who are much too ready to think evil of themselves and to distress themselves with their evil thinking. It is better not to appraise one's own spiritual life and progress, but to leave it to God and to band all attention to advancing in love of God and love of neighbor.

From another point of view, it is true that the witness of our heart is not always reliable, and we sometimes have to appeal to God against our own hearts. Saul of Tarsus was very conscientious in his fierce persecution of the early Christians. "I verily thought with myself, that I ought to do many things contrary to the Name of Jesus of Nazareth." There are some who boast that they have a good conscience, but in those who have given themselves to many excesses, this could really be a state that is called "past feeling" or a conscience that has been "seared with a hot iron." Many a conscience, wearied and exhausted through ineffectual remonstrances, eventually loses its sensitivity and becomes totally obdurate.

The person who has a good conscience, even though he has had many sins, always has confidence in God. Our absolution by conscience is not infallible. The conscience is probably much more reliable when it condemns than when it acquits. One is always on the safe side when he follows conscience when it says, "You are wrong," but he is not always vindicated when his conscience says, "You are right." The inward judge needs to be stimulated and enlightened and kept under the guidance of the spirit.

When Peter was told to throw his nets into the

sea after having unsuccessfully fished all night, he said that he would obey the will of the Master. He lowered his nets and, so great was the catch of fish, that the nets began to tear. He then changed the word Master to Lord and asked pardon saying, "Depart from me, O Lord, for I am a sinful man."

The consciousness of sin rushed upon him at once as a consequence of that new invasion of the Divine. He now saw his own hollowness and evil and had a desire to be forgiven. There comes to every man an awakening of conscience, sometimes at the sight of an infant, or a sickness, or a chance word, or a personal sorrow. For one split second there is a glimpse of the purity and holiness and nearness of God, compared to which we appear unholy, but are never in despair. When the heart accuses, God is greater than the heart.

## Harmony of the Whole Person

Those whose minds think only about one subject are like those who use only one set of muscles in the body. In one instance, there is incomplete mental development; in the other, incomplete physical development. The bow must sometimes be unbent, the crops must be rotated and, in the name of inner peace and quiet, a protest must be raised against unceasing and exclusive occupation with things. Our lamps must be fed secretly with holy oil. As one of the greatest of the European psychiatrists has said, "It is as if in a beehive one section of the bees followed the Divine purpose dictated to them by their instincts, while others departed from it. One might indeed describe such a hive as diseased. That is why to seek in prayer the purpose of God for our lives, and to enjoy personal fellowship with Christ Who delivers us from the things that stand in the way of that purpose, leads to that harmony of the whole person which is one of the prerequisites of health."

The growth of character could very largely be the discovery that the things we thought innocent once are no longer innocent. The more saintly a person becomes, the more he feels himself a sinner. That is because he judges himself not by worldly standards nor by his weak neighbors, but by God Himself. Nothing is more clearly witnessed by individual experience than that we may do a wrong thing and think that it is right. Our Blessed Lord said, "They will kill you and think that they have done a service to God." A few honest moments of self-searching would reveal to the man who boasts that he has never done wrong, that his feelings would be quite different if he stood before the Throne of Divine Justice, holding out press clippings and pointing to a few marble busts in field-houses and copper plates in gymnasiums.

Years ago, when I was a student in Europe, I followed for a time the very popular courses in Paris of Henri Bergson, the famous philosopher. It was in vogue to attend his lectures; one would often see parked in front of the Collège de France the finest of European automobiles, from which descended ladies who were keeping up with the latest philosophical fashion. The popularity of Bergson in those days, however, did not blind others to the great value of his thought. The basic idea of his system was an attack upon reason and intellect. He felt that it did not give a complete insight into life, simply because life eludes all analysis. A wheat field, he said, could not be described merely by taking a straw, putting it on a paper card, and showing it to students.

No one has arisen in our age to play the same role in psychology that Bergson played in philosophy, namely, to crack down on the analysis which smashes human beings as if they were atoms, but can never put them together again. Sigmund Freud made psychoanalysis very popular, and in doing so, gave to the world insights into the depths of the mind which too long had been ignored. It could very well be that there has been such an emphasis or stress on psychoanalysis as to ignore the hidden syntheses of his thought. A distinguished Swiss psychiatrist made an analysis of the 260 clinical cases which Freud quotes in his book *The Psychopathology of Everyday Life*. All, without exception, would be classified in one or another of the four categories of sin described in the Sermon on the Mount: 57 are concerned with dishonesty; 39 with impurity; 122 with self-centeredness or egotism; and 42 with lack of love of neighbor.

Could it not be that all this analysis of the psychic life of the person is but the inverse of a synthesis which every peaceless heart seeks? Freud was actually describing what St. Paul long before had observed, namely, that within every man is a conflict of the law of the flesh and the law of the spirit. Ovid too had traced it in saying that everyone seeks the better things of life, but often follows that which is worse.

Is not the time ripe for someone to develop a psychology based on a synthesis or a unifying of the presently discordant and battling forces inside of man? Actually we are on the thin edge of that consolidation of the broken fragments of the mind and heart. While there always remains a certain number of mental aberrations which can be healed only by analysis on the psychological level, there are also many more aberrations of a moral character which can be healed only at the moral level. It costs considerable money to tell one's complexes to a psychoanalyst; it costs only pride and arrogance of soul to confess our sins to representatives of the moral and Divine order. The fact that we conceal sins makes them peculiarly our own. Then they are not just our fault; they are our very penalty. Any concealed fault lays a heavy burden on the soul over and above the remorse for the sin itself. The shame of having hid it in the heart always makes the hider feel as if he were acting a lie; he despises himself in the midst of every word of praise that he receives. A confession to a neighbor whom we have wronged is prescribed as the very condition of our receiving pardon. God accepts no service or worship with our hands until we have confessed the wrong done to others.

# NEIGHBORLINESS

## Who Is My Neighbor?

Very often a neighbor is regarded as one who lives next door, or in the same block, or in an adjoining apartment.

Once Our Lord was asked by a lawyer, "Who is my neighbor?" Our Blessed Lord answered by telling him a parable: There was a man who went down from Jerusalem to Jericho, fell among thieves, was stripped of his garments, wounded and left half dead. The road that leads down from Jerusalem to Jericho covers a distance of twenty-one miles and it was known, because of its dark deeds, as "the way of blood."

Our Lord told how the priest and the Levite passed by — a proof of the degenerate state into which religion had fallen. Perhaps, in modern language, they went down to Jericho to report to some philanthropic association that a man was wounded on the road midway between Jerusalem and Jericho.

A Samaritan, who was of another race, bound up the wounds of the injured man, poured in oil and wine, set him on his beast and brought him to an inn. He paid the innkeeper and promised to return again to pay for additional expenses.

When Our Blessed Lord asked the lawyer who was the neighbor, he would not say the Samaritan, because he was not permitted to say the word. He merely answered that the neighbor was "the one who showed mercy." Our Blessed Lord then told him to go and do likewise.

Our Lord made neighborhood coextensive with humanity. Any human being is a neighbor who needs aid or to whom one can render aid. A neighbor is not one bound by the same race, nor is he the one close to us. He may be the one farthest away; he could even be an enemy.

Very often misery is unrelieved because it is not clamorous. When we hear of great numbers of people lying half dead on the roadside, the very magnitude of their need is apt to make us feel that we can do little and, therefore, might be excused from doing anything.

We are to make use of things — our possessions, our talents — as kinds of sacraments, each one of which has pronounced over it the consecrating words: "This is offered on account of You, O Lord!" Thus the whole universe can become sacramentalized for His honor and glory. Even those in the dim borderland of acquaintance — the chance passerby on the road, the one whom we have never seen before — all possess a quality that identifies them even with another Traveler Who one day sat tired at Jacob's well: "Whatever you did for one of these least brothers of Mine, you did for Me."

## *Two Sides of Sympathy*

What has happened to that double side of sympathy which is the basis of the Christian philosophy of life: "Rejoice with those who rejoice, and weep with those who weep"? It has been said that the wounded deer sheds tears, but it belongs only to man to weep with those who weep and by sympathy to divide another's sorrows and double another's joys.

In a nation, bad blood arises immediately when others are indifferent to our misfortunes. Nothing so spoils a people as a spirit which makes each say, "I am I and you are you, and that's the end of it." Rather, as the poet said:

> *We, are we not formed as notes of music are*
> *For one another though dissimilar?*

Of the two kinds of sympathy, it seems easier to show sympathy with people in trouble than to rejoice with happy folk. In Shakespeare's *As You Like It*, there is a description of two brothers, each in love with his chosen mistress. One succeeds in his courtship, whereupon the other exclaims, "How bitter it is to look into happiness through another man's eyes!"

Furthermore, it seems to be easier to do one of these than to do both together. Some are more sensitive to pain in others, and others are more sensitive to joy in others. It could be that, feeling the need of sympathy ourselves, we play a sympathetic tune on the keyboard of another; but why, it might be asked, since we all wish joy, not share in another's joy?

It has been said that it becomes easier to do both as we grow older. One of the heroes of Homer sang:

> Taught by time, my heart has learned to glow
> For others' good and weep at others' woe.

Every man rejoices twice when he has a partner in his joy. He who shares tears with us wipes them away. He divides them in two, and he who laughs with us makes the joy double. Two torches do not divide, but increase the flame. Tears are more quickly dried up when they run on a friend's cheek in furrows of compassion.

How beautifully both these sympathies were revealed in the character of Our Blessed Lord when He saw the leper, the widow of Naim, the blind man by the wayside, the hungry multitudes distressed "as sheep without a shepherd." He touched the leper; He dried the tears of the widow; He was hungry with the hungry and He fed them. He suffered with their suffering. One day a publican made a great feast in his house. Our Lord sat down with His disciples, saying that while the Bridegroom was with them, they should all rejoice. He also entered sympathetically into the joys of the marriage feast of Cana, making better wine even when the poor wine had been drained.

Few there are who can carry this sympathy to a point of forgiveness as Our Lord did from the Cross; as St. Thomas More, Chancellor of England, did when he gave a blessing to his persecutors. Just before being killed, he was asked if he had anything to say. His answer was, "My lords, I have but to say that as the blessed Apostle St. Paul was present at the death of the martyr, Stephen, keeping the clothes of those who stoned him, and yet they be now saints in Heaven, and there shall continue to be friends forever, so I trust and shall, therefore, pray, that though your lordships have been on earth my judges, yet we may hereafter meet in Heaven together to our everlasting salvation: and God preserve you all, especially our sovereign lord, the king, and grant him faithful counsellors."

## Politeness

Politeness is passing out of the world. Some never think of it as being anything else than offering a seat to a lady when one gets off the bus. Not very long ago, a man stood up on the subway and offered his vacated seat to a lady. She fainted in surprise. When she recovered and sat down, she thanked the man, and he fainted.

Taking account of American hurry and rush, someone has defined courtesy as a form of polite behavior practiced by civilized people when they have time. In the last century, when there was much talk about a gentleman, someone defined a gentleman as the "devil's imitation of a Christian."

That brings up the question: What is, according to Scripture, the essence of a Christian gentleman? There are two tests which are given.

One is: "Be patient in bearing with one another's fault as charity bids." This means a restraining of displeasure against annoyance or insult, or the power of bearing up under offenses. It sometimes requires great moral and spiritual strength to overcome the desire for retaliation which is in the natural man. To be a Christian gentleman who follows the example of Christ, who, when He was reviled, reviled not again, and when He suffered, threatened not, is indeed difficult. Stoicism ignores the faults of others, but the Christian gentleman is directed to forgive them by loving.

The other test of the gentleman is in following the counsel of Our Blessed Lord, to go and sit in the lowest place, and not the highest. There is always false ambition when a man aims at a place rather than merit. A well-known modern French novelist, writing about her relations with another well-known character, often writes this sentence: "I got the corner seat," or "we got the corner seats." Dozens of toes were probably trampled upon because here there was vanity and self-seeking. It can generally be found that this false ambition is due not to the fact that they are truly great, but rather that they are small and have not learned to manage themselves.

The gentleman is the one who is modest and retiring, who waits first on the others and thinks of everyone but himself, and finds his chief happiness in making someone else happy; who, however poor and humble anyone else may be, bears to them the open palm of true nobility.

In the story of the Gospel feast, it was the man who sought the higher place who was sent to the lower, and then one who took the lower place who was sent up higher. In the world, there is push and rush; in the audits of Heaven, the emptying of the ego is a condition of admittance of God's action within the soul.

It would, of course, be quite wrong to say that we should appear humble. One often hears speakers at banquets, when they are given some cup, or diploma, or degree, or praise, answer, "I am very humble, but proud" — without ever thinking of how they could be both at the same time. Humility is like underwear: we have to have it, but we should never show it. Pride is what we think ourselves to be; humility is the truth we know about ourselves, not in the eyes of our neighbor, but in the eyes of God.

As Chesterton put it, "There is no such thing as being a gentleman at important moments; it is at unimportant moments that a man is a gentleman.... If once his mind is possessed in any strong degree with the knowledge that he is a gentleman, he will soon cease to be one."

## Honesty

Abraham Lincoln once said, "If, in your judgment, you cannot be an honest lawyer, resolve to be honest without being a lawyer."

It has often been said, "Honesty is the best policy," on the grounds that it will keep you out of trouble and make you admired. Someone has re-marked concerning it, "He who acts upon this principle is not an honest man." It would seem, however, that there is some decline in honesty, for there is now one major crime committed in the United States for every sixty persons. In the last ten years, the crime rate in the United States has been exploding at a rate four times as fast as the rate of the growth of our population.

The justification for cutting corners, taking bribes and other forms of dishonesty is twofold. First is, "Everybody's doing it." The assumption here is that right and wrong are questions merely of mob judgment, rather than of standards. It forgets that right is right if nobody is right, and wrong is wrong if everybody is wrong. A second justification is, "My conscience is clear." What conscience is not clear if it makes its own standards? What note on a piano is wrong if the musician who strikes it declares it to be the right note? If a conscience decides that eighteen inches will be a yard, who shall prove him wrong? The atheistic Khrushchev, with all the crimes of the Ukraine on his back, said, "God knows I do right."

Every act of dishonesty disturbs the balance of justice and, therefore, demands restitution. The old law of Moses on stealing was, "If he is found guilty, he must make restitution, giving back in full all that he hoped to gain by his knavery, and a fifth part beside, to the owner whom he has wronged."

Zacchaeus was a public servant of the Romans, a tax gatherer who paid a large sum for his office. Part of the taxes he would give to the Romans, but he pocketed all he collected over the amount due them. Unless his exactions were too ruinous, there was little fear of exposure. But one day he was checked in his dishonesty, not by having it exposed in the press of the times, nor by having the prosecuting attorney of the Romans bring him to halt. He was "arrested" by the moral stringency of Our Divine Lord, Whose awful eyes pierced his soul and made him seek not only pardon, but also render restitution. Standing upright, he said, "Lord, here and now I give half of what I have to the poor; if I have wronged anyone in any way, I make restitution of it fourfold."

We once received a plain, brown envelope in which there was stuffed $4,600 in bills, and to which was attached an anonymous note to the effect that the sender was making reparation for his dishonesty to an insurance company, the name and address of which was given. We sent the money to the insurance company and told them of the unjust claim that had been made against them, but the name of the one who had made the restitution remained unknown. Regardless of how much one may have taken, and regardless of how secretly it may have been done, and regardless of how one may have justified it in his own false conscience, the Divine words still stand: "Believe Me, you will not be released until you have paid the last penny."

## *Success and Failure*

A spoiled life may sometimes be a spur; a successful life may sometimes be a drag. Success is never a success when measured wholly in terms of dollars. Life is a becoming, rather than a having; a goal in front, and not an achievement. The poet has said, "Beware of the man of one book," for he is always talking about it, instead of proceeding to write another.

Those who boast of their success are not successful, and those who pride themselves on their perfection are not saints. From this, there follow two psychological observations.

First, it will generally be found true that those who boast of their success in terms of money hardly ever help the poor. It is not that they are not generous, but that they are generous only to the rich. The haves are helped by those who have; it is the have-nots who help the have-nots. An institution worth half a billion dollars can easily get endowments and have drives for a hundred million dollars, but the ten million lepers in the world are lucky if they draw three hundred thousand dollars a year from pockets — but not from the same pockets. What is the reason for this? It is partly because the rich measure their own lives in terms of success, and so they think that only those causes should be helped which are also successful. Furthermore, always having had the "breaks" and good fortune, they are incapable of understanding the want and the misery of others. That is why the poor are more generous to the poor — because they know hunger, they give the little bread they have.

This brings us to the other psychological law governing perfection: the pharisaically perfect who have not known human weakness are often less sympathetic and less helpful to the fallen than those who, with the grace of God, have picked themselves up from the mire. It was the Pharisee who sneered at the Lord when the adulterous woman came to pour ointment on His feet. He could not understand why Perfection did not pick up His robes from such filth. St. Augustine, who was a great sinner, was a more understanding theologian of the grace and mercy of God than St. Thomas, who had so few human weaknesses. Parents who boast of their moral uprightness can rarely sympathize with the weakness of their children; they too often make virtue repulsive instead of attractive. The description of Christ in the Bible is the ideal: "We do not have a High Priest Who is unable to sympathize with our weaknesses, but One Who has been tempted in every way as we are, yet remained without sin." True innocence is compassionate.

It is interesting to note the difference between missionaries and spoiled modern youths who have had everything. The first have often been through every conceivable kind of trial — poverty, hunger, deprivation, sometimes even prison, torture, and death — and yet they are the happiest persons who ever lived. Never does one hear them say a harsh word against those who have made their lives difficult. They hate oppression, but they love their oppressors simply because they are human. Over-privileged youths, on the contrary, are often bored, jaded, sour at life, and bent on destruction because they have destroyed their own inner image of the Divine. The professor of moral theology and of canon law will generally be found to be less sympathetic to human weakness than the priest or minister or rabbi who works in the slums, or with delinquents, and certainly less merciful than the one who is truly saintly, for he above all knows how weak he is.

Those who are patient under trial are those who are most capable of consoling others; those who are rebellious under crosses can never bring comfort to the afflicted. The sinless people who are boastful of their goodness are always harsh, and sinful people who remain in their sin are often indifferent to goodness and justice. But those who are dissatisfied with their goodness, and strive to perfect the Divine Image within, are always sympathetic and compassionate. A successful life can be a spoiled life if it is summed up in "I made millions."

A spoiled life, on the contrary, need not be a hopeless life. Failures if properly accepted can lead to true success. Abraham Lincoln was defeated for every public office until he was elected President. Einstein was expelled from a school in Munich because he showed no interest in his studies and later failed to pass his test for a polytechnic school. A cross seen as the Will of God leads to an Easter Sunday.

## My Brother's Keeper

The first recorded question that man hurled back into the Face of God was, "Am I my brother's keeper?" Cain had brought the first death into the world by killing Abel. God, seeking to arouse his conscience, asked, "Where is your brother Abel?" His conscience was already dead, but he tried to escape his guilt with the retort, "Am I my brother's keeper?"

How God spoke we know not, except that He accommodated Himself to the conscience of Cain. What now becomes interesting is that having failed to induce Cain to acknowledge his guilt, God looked elsewhere for evidence to convict him.

Cain had already put himself in the position of those today who deny that there is any such thing as guilt or sin. The great novelist Dostoevski foretold that this would come to pass in the modern world, saying, "A time will come when men will say there is no sin, there is no crime, there is no guilt. There is only hunger. And men will come to our feet crying and imploring: 'Give us bread.'"

In this state of denial of personal guilt and responsibility, Cain was at the same time denying that he had any responsibility to society. There seems to be an intrinsic bond between man's denial of personal moral failure and his repudiation of involvement with the ills and woes of others.

Dostoevski, again stressing the contrary view, says, "Think of yourself as being responsible for the sins of your fellowmen, and you will see how quickly you will want to relieve their burdens."

Following the marvelous psychological insights in the story, God answers the question of Cain, "Am I my brother's keeper?" by saying, "Your brother's blood cries out to Me from the soil." Even though Cain refused to hear the whisper of conscience or, better, the questioning voice of God, inanimate nature itself protested. Nature is on God's side, not on man's.

Something of this mystery is hidden in the prophecy of Our Lord to Peter, that there would be a link between Peter's denial of Him and the crowing of a cock. In the absence of accusation from our fellow beings, all visible creation — sun, moon, stars, forest, water — seems to grow vocal to publish our crime. It is likely that the very branches of the tree on which Judas hanged himself seemed to him like pointing fingers. Thompson's words concerning nature were, "Traitorous trueness, loyal deceit. In fickleness to me and in loyalty to Him." When the dialogue which conscience holds with the guilty is rejected, the universe itself becomes a mirror, holding crime up for all to see.

Could it be that because a man has evolved out of the dust into which God breathed an immortal soul, then the wrong that is done echoes and reverberates throughout the vast realm of nature? In any case, there is a sympathy between the moral order and the physical, between conscience and the human body, between the moral and the somatic. Could one not translate nature's declaring Cain's sin into modern psychological terms? How often those who are morally guilty and who deny their guilt might hear God's voice in new ways saying, "Your sins cried out to Me from your psychosis, your neurosis and your dreams. The guilt that you deny is not effaced; it is merely submerged. And though you have not permitted Me to read it in your conscience, I read it in your nerves, in your complexes, in the very ground of your being."

Perhaps Cain had concealed beneath the sod the blood of his brother and, with the greatest attention, removed every visible trace to the superficial examiner of his foul deed. He had learned that the things which he thought dumb could raise their voices to the ear of Omnipotence, and that the blood of a brother which he shed could rise vocal with words of prayer. Many a misdeed in theft and adultery, buried under the sod of the conscious mind, has its voice too. Every psychic disturbance which is the result of thumbing one's nose against the moral order also has its voice. It is not the ground today but the mental ills which cry out to Heaven. Nature confirms and illustrates in every particular the unconfessed and the unpardoned guilt which has its record in the body and in the mind, and cries out to Heaven from that ground "with crimson clouds before their eyes and flames about their brain."

## The Strong and the Weak

If one plants a rose tree in the shadow of an oleander, the oleander will fatten on the life of the rose tree, which eventually dies from what has been taken away from it. The weak succumbs to the strong. The grip of the vine is on all the feeble plants of the field. Wolves often rend in pieces a wounded member of their pack. The lion devours the lamb and grows stronger by absorbing the strength of the vanquished. Written across the law of nature is "the survival of the fittest." Even in the international order, weaker nations have succumbed one by one — devoured by the stronger.

But there is another law that is not in nature, at least not in raw nature, namely, "We who are strong should bear the infirmities of the weak and not please ourselves." It is here that Christianity makes its most unique and distinctive pronouncement, and gives the supreme example of Divinity dying for the weakness and sinfulness of humanity. The Christian law is not "the survival of the fittest" but "the survival of the unfit."

The inspiration for this is He Who emptied Himself of Heaven's wealth that through His poverty we might be made rich. The challenge was uttered to the Cross: "Come down and we will believe." But He did not come down. If He had come down, He would have been strong. He stayed there. He would die for the weak. Through that act of self-denial, the unfit lived.

All during His Life, love went out to those who were not only weak, but even the worst people, like the woman in the city, the grasping tax collector, the robber on the tree. He saw that a jewel had fallen into the mud and though encrusted with foulness that it was still a jewel.

Strength is apt to please itself. And health is

prone to claim immunity from sympathy with pain. But according to this law, the man with eyes must be a staff to those who are blind. Virtuous innocence never claims immunity from the guilt of others. That is why an innocent woman was found at the foot of the Cross. The truest sympathy is found in those who, with the strength of love, come out of the sunshine into the gloom and dimness of others, to touch wounds tenderly, as though their own nerves throbbed with pain.

The burden is on the strong. The fit must minister to the unfit; the rich must aid the poor. The blind man who tramples our flowers is not to be the object of toleration; rather, the loss of his sight must be felt by us as a personal loss. How often today writers and novelists take on the air of supporting the weak, the poor and the disinherited, but how few ever give any of their royalties to assist those whose misery made their fortune. The slum owner is often brought before the law for making money on hovels, but does the novelist who made a fortune on slums ever share his reward with them? Really, only they who themselves have suffered are the strong who help the weak.

Hugo Bassi tries to lift others to that insight in his lines:

*Measure thy life by loss instead of gain;*
*Not by the wine drunk but the wine poured forth;*

*For love's strength standeth in love's sacrifice;*
*And who so suffers most hath most to give.*

## Judging Others

Human nature is something like a child's top painted in the variegated colors of the rainbow. When the top is at rest, each single color and tint can be distinguished, the red on one side, blue on another, white on the top, green on the bottom. When the top is set in motion and made to spin, darkness is suffused with brightness, brightness is mixed with darkness, the colors melt into a confused gray until at last one knows not what hues it be.

Judging our fellow men is as perplexing as the perceiving of colors on a spinning top. When a man is at rest, or in a fixed state, such as playing a game or working at a lathe, we think we can very well judge his character. But when we see him in the whirl and motion of everyday life, with its incessant change of pace, its rapid flash from one occupation or duty to another, all his goodness and badness blur into indistinctness. There is so much goodness at one moment, badness at another, sin in one instance, virtue in another, sobriety at one post, excess in another, that it is well to leave the judgment to

God and to give the most charitable interpretation one can.

As Robert Burns wrote, begging that there be not severe judgment of his fellow man:

> *Who made the heart, 'tis He alone*
> *Decidedly can try us;*
> *He knows each chord, its various tone,*
> *Each spring, its various bias:*
> *Then at the balance let's be mute,*
> *We never can adjust it;*
> *What's done we partly may compute,*
> *But know not what's resisted.*

Our Blessed Lord gave us one standard by which others may be judged; it was not a positive, but a negative one. "Judge not, and you shall not be judged. For as you judge, so will you be judged, and the measure with which you measure will be measured out to you."

The way we judge others is very often the judgment which we pronounce upon ourselves. Whenever you find anyone who is hateful, censorious and bitter against those who lead religious lives, inquire not into his intellectual background; rather investigate his behavior. Those who condemned severely the woman in the Gospel and used her as a test case of the Mercy of Our Lord were themselves guilty of adultery. In all judgments, it is never so important to inquire *what* is said, but *why* it is said.

Every dramatist, scriptwriter, novelist and essayist who attacks the moral law has already lived against it in his own life. These men may not know it, but in their writings they are penning their own autobiographies. Those who satirize decency, who pour vitriolic acid on family life, who excuse militant atheism, are in the language of a poet "but a clod of warmer dust mixed with cunning sparks from hell."

Nero thought no person chaste because he was so unchaste himself. On the other hand, it will be found that those who are the most religious are those who are the least censorious. A legend has it that one day an ambassador of God severely reprimanded a penitent. The former heard coming from the Crucifix the words, "*I died for his sins, not you.*" It will invariably be found true that those who have suffered and who are saintly are always the most merciful to others. Not to be forgotten also are those who have received mercy and forgiveness themselves. One wonders if Saint Augustine was not one of the kindest and most compassionate of men, having been so tenderly touched by mercy after his sinful life.

Adelaide Ann Proctor, pleading for a sympathetic understanding of souls who have fallen, writes:

> *The fall thou darest to despise —*
> *May be the angel's slackened hand*
> *Has suffered it, that he may rise*

*And take a firmer, sterner stand;*
*Or, trusting less to earthly things*
*May henceforth learn to use his wings.*

## Understanding Others

The Good Samaritan has stood for centuries as the supreme example of one who had compassion on his fellow man. The word itself means "to suffer with" the afflicted, the poor, the hungry and the thirsty.

The new compassion that has crept into our courts and into our literature and drama is the compassion for the breakers of the law, for the thieves, the drug dealers, the murderers, the rapists. This false compassion for the criminal and the readiness to blame the law and the police, has passed from the "sob sisters" to black-robed justices who, fearful of restraining a liberty turned into license, pardon the mugger and ignore the mugged.

This miscarriage of justice is found also in the inability of the prosperous to understand the unfortunate. The woes of widows, mothers with delinquent children and cancer patients are often beyond the comprehension of would-be sympathizers. They think that they have sounded all depths and therefore are in a position to judge the merits of the one who is in agony. They have merely skimmed the surface. They do not know what others suffer; neither do they understand God's plan in relationship to them. Looking from sunny homes on the dark abodes of misery, they cannot understand the sorrows they have never tasted. Always having had their wants satisfied, they do not know the meaning of hunger and thirst.

It is part of our fallen nature to despise the trouble we do not understand. Not having the power to drive into the mystery, it seems to us a shallow thing. When the sufferers complain much, we are inclined to think that they are exaggerating or giving way to cowardly weakness, just as the rich are too often ready to regard the very poor as whining imposters. He who has never felt the pangs of conscience looks with contempt upon the penitent's tears. The Pharisees were very unmerciful to sinners, but a great sinner like Augustine could understand them well. When one is looking for counsel, it is always well to seek out those who themselves have suffered. There is much more wisdom resulting from patient bearing of suffering than there is from books. No sinner is ever consoled by having a moral theology flung at his head. Perhaps the reason why Peter and not John was chosen as the Head of the Church was because he fell and, therefore, understood human weakness. Suffering may be sent to us because we have been too narrow and selfish in our view of it, and also to prepare us for our work in helping others in trouble. The widow can sympathize with the widow; the poor show most kindness to the poor. The experience of the prostration of a great illness enables a person to understand and help sick people. Sorrow can thus become a talent to be used for the good of others by being invested in sympathy.

The principal reason why Christ suffered was to make Him not only our Savior, but also our Sorrows: "He was a Man of Sorrow and acquainted with grief." Hence the sufferer who is despised by his prosperous brethren can turn with assurance of sympathy to the Savior of men. Our Lord learned compassion by what He suffered and thereby converted the Cross into a lever for raising a fallen world. Those who receive mercy from Him should show mercy; those who owe all they have to the pity of God, will not be pitiless to their brethren. The Savior never for a moment tolerates that self-righteous isolation which would make us despise the Prodigal, cavil at his restoration, or cry out with the spirit of Cain, "Am I my brother's keeper?"

## Passing By

What does the Gospel mean when it says, describing the Risen Lord's appearance at Emmaus, "He gave the impression that He was going on farther; but they urged Him to stay with them"? It means that Our Lord passes us by each day in every opportunity to do good. If we neglect the opportunity, He does not reveal Himself. When the false Christ comes he will say, "I am the Christ." But not so with the Divine Christ. He seems to walk by us, trying our dim eyes and weak hands to see if we have faith enough to want Him to stay with us. He leaves us in darkness if we ask not for the Light. Never does He act independently of our desires for intimate union with Him. He breaks down no doors; the latch is on our side. He stands without the door and knocks.

He has "no place to lay His Head" unless a friendly soul, like the friends at Bethany, give Him lodging. The innkeeper at Bethlehem missed the opportunity of forever saying of his inn, "Jesus was born here." "I was a stranger and you took Me in," He will say on the Last Day, but He will be only a stranger to those who did not press the invitation.

This same principle of hiding until sought after is evident throughout His life. At Jericho there was a blind man by the name of Bartimaeus who kept crying out, "Jesus, Son of David, have pity on me." The Lord pretended to pass him by, but despite the rebuke even of others in the crowd the blind man cried out more loudly and was cured.

So it was with the woman who came from the neighborhood of Tyre and Sidon and pleaded that He cure her ailing daughter, who was troubled by an evil spirit; He gave her no word in answer. His disciples came to Him and pleaded with Him. "Rid us of her," they said. But after further testing her faith, He answered her, "Woman, great is your faith! Let it be done for you as you wish." And from that hour, her daughter was cured.

Every word that comes to us about the uncomfortable, the homeless, the lepers, is the Son of God passing by. If we let Him pass, He may never be recalled. Graces unused are not often repeated; whispers ignored do not become shouts. All through life, our hands will stretch forth empty of the richest blessings of wisdom and truth unless they are first used to clutch at the sleeve of the Divine Who gives the impression that He would pass us by. Emotional responsiveness without practical issue harms the soul. The drama stirs the emotions, but awakens no duties toward the afflicted on the stage. For the moment we may feel we are on the side of the angels. But that is what the Romans called *ignis fatuus* — the empty fire — the pleasurable glow that consumes no evil and illumines no path.

DOCTRINES AND NATIONS

## Is God Dead?

Humanity might well pause in these days when the hot flames of hell, by a peculiar paradox, fan a cold war of prejudice and hate. Digging deeper than politics and economics, what is the path modern man is taking? Without knowing it, he has, in practice, accepted the dictum of Nietzsche: "God is dead." This death of God is not a physical demise, due to such things as nailing Him to a gibbet; it is much less dramatic. It means simply that the idea of God has disappeared among men. He is only a name, a "survival," "a remnant" of other days, according to some misbehaviorists. "God is dead" means He can be ignored, as one ignores the necessity of a horse and buggy for transportation because the automobile has taken its place. The new vehicle for progress is "humanity."

Atheism has moved from the intellectual plane, where it was in the nineteenth century, to the existential plane; from the level of proving atheism to the living it; from the nonexistence of God to the existence of humanity. Atheism posits a new god, namely, Man. The position of Marx and Engels, the founders of Communism, is that man has transferred to God qualities and attributes which really belong to man, such as knowing all things, possessing power to do all things, unlimited compassion, unbounded love and torrential mercy. Man, they continue, has destroyed his nature by this transfer of attributes to God; thus he emptied himself. The only way he can ever be himself is to take back those titles which really belong to him. Then will be ushered into the world that humanism in which Man is God and not mere man. Atheism then becomes not the denial of God but the affirmation of Man. Marx wrote at the end of his thesis for a Ph.D., "I hate all the gods, and I hate them because they do not recognize Man as Supreme Divinity."

Official atheism, such as was put into practice in Marxism, implies an entirely new concept of truth. For those who believe in God, truth is conformity: (a) with the objective, natural order revealed in the universe and in conscience, and (b) ultimately with the Mind that made it. For example, my idea of a rose corresponds to a certain type of flower in the physical order. I do not say, "My idea of a rose is an elephant." In the ultimate analysis, just as a statue corresponds to an idea or plan existing in the mind of the sculptor, so every rose, tree, bird and stone corresponds to an idea existing in the Mind of God. Deny God, and what is truth? Truth, under atheism, is correspondence or agreement with an idea existing in the collective mind of the ruling elite. Reality must correspond to the archetypal ideas existing in the mind of the humanist planners. Black is white and white is black; day is night and night is day. As Marx said, every idea is "true" which furthers the revolution, and false which hinders it. There is no objective standard of truth. One's cause alone is truth. This explains why atheistic political leaders can appear to be so good and democratic and freedom loving one day, and so cantankerous, deceitful and full of lies another day. Both tactics are "true." It is the cause that counts.

In the face of a kind of atheism that does not prove itself, all the intellectual arguments in the world for theism lack the power to convince. If a balloon were conscious, it would be pretty hard for a vacuum to induce it to deflate itself. Man who is god does not want to be man. He likes the beautiful irresponsibility of his excesses; he loves to hear the word compulsion to explain away his alcoholism. What then will convince the atheist and humanist of today that he is not the lord and sovereign of the universe?

One thing which atheism brings is chaos. Sociologists and psychologists, politicians and historians would do well to read the first chapter of Paul's Letter to the Romans for the consequences of human pride. We quote it not, in the hope that the reader will pursue it himself. It may sharpen his curiosity if he is told that the explanation for many of our modern-day problems is recorded therein. Our troubles are not really outside us; they are within. Nothing happens in the world that does not first happen in human hearts.

## Economics

In his play, *Magic*, G.K. Chesterton tells of a duke who signed two checks. One check was to aid in the building of a large saloon; the second check was to aid the league opposing the building of the saloon. It was not long until he had the reputation of being a "very liberal-minded man."

Economics begins with having. Economics has something to do with having. Having is a sign of imperfection. The purpose of having is to remedy our incompleteness. If we had perfect life, we would never need nourishment. Because our knowledge is imperfect, we need to complement it with education. Because our personality is inadequate for happiness, we need love.

It was creation that introduced the verb "have." When there was only God, before the world was made, there was only one verb, and only one form of the verb — namely, the infinitive "to be" — to indicate the Supreme being of God. God has nothing, but because He is sheer being, He is infinitely rich. If God had anything, it would be a sign that He needed something external to Himself in order to perfect His being.

But all possessions are extrinsic to us; they are never really a part of ourselves. It is, therefore, very easy to confuse having with being. We think we are something because we have something. On Judgment Day we will be judged only by being and not by having. The only things that we will be able to take with us will be those that we can take in a shipwreck. When an honest motorcycle policeman stops us on the highway, he does not ask what kind of car we are driving, but whether or not we obeyed the law. Man can be aggressive in acquiring. Man can be voluptuous in possessing. Man can be avaricious in retaining.

Since property has to do with having, there are two kinds of property: real and token. Real property consists of something physical and concrete which is related to use — for example, beds, land, ice cream, cabbage, corn, spinach, wagons. Token property is an artifice to express reality. Token wealth consists of stocks, bonds, money that has been folded and money that has not been folded.

Nature sets a limit to real wealth or property. No man desires an infinite meal or an infinite garment, or an infinite garden. A garden is a garden only when it has limits and therefore begets peace and complacency. Nature sets limits to the real wealth that we can use. There is a limit to the number of beds we can have in a room, a limit to the ice cream a boy can eat. One boy said that he never has too much ice cream; there just is not enough stomach. In Australia some of the primitive peoples count up to three. They say, "One, two, three enough." This is because they have no refrigerators and cannot keep their food longer than three days. Agriculture has, therefore, been considered one of the most peaceful enterprises of man, because man works with nature and nature sets limits to production and, therefore, to consumption.

Token wealth, however, is to a great extent infinite, simply because it is a symbol of something else. Avarice for credit tends toward infinity because it evokes an infinite desire. Though tokens do not fill the heart, they do fill the time. In real wealth a person limits his wealth by needs, but in token wealth the average person cannot be trusted to accumulate only sufficient tokens to satisfy his needs. Just as there are chain smokers, so there are chain hotels, chain grocery stores, chain railroads. In the language of the Gospel, a man builds bigger and bigger barns until the recording angel summons him to judgment.

## Influence

Influence is that which a man is, the sum total of all his beliefs, actions, goals, habits, values, affections, manifested in all he does and does not. Influence is almost the opposite of a photograph; in the latter, an impression of the outside world is made upon a film. With influence, it is the photographer himself who impresses his imprint on another person. Because the light is in him, it shines on others; because the glow is in him, he radiates love. Influence is something like the shadow of Peter which cured the sick. As evil men spread immoral germs and infect the substance of another man's character, so there are those, like Peter, who cast shadows of beneficent healing, and who leave in the gallery of memory the portrait of one who does lasting spiritual good.

A second point about influence is that those who exercise it are quite apart from the masses and the mobs. Mediocre and weak characters succumb to the moods and fashions of the moment. Dead logs float downstream; it takes a live swimmer to resist the current. The creative element in any society is always a minority. There are multitudes in every organization, but the great influences are singular and almost unique. Those seeking to change society use the right principle when they seek to train a revolutionary core or elite. In this they are imitating Christ, Who chose out of the multitude first one man, then three, then twelve, then seventy, to change the world.

Who was it who delivered Israel from the Philistines? It was a solitary Samson, and in another instance, a solitary David with his stone and sling-shot. Who was it who gathered the people together to rout the Midianites? It was Gideon. And the Lord told him to reduce his army to a mere three hundred, for those three hundred would have more influence than thirty thousand.

A final reflection is that sometimes great influences are exercised by those who once were evil and abandoned it. Not only the unspoiled saints, but the saints who have been converted from wrong, are potent forces of good. The night of the Last Supper, Our Lord told Peter, "Simon, Simon, behold, Satan has demanded to sift all of you like wheat, but I have prayed that your own faith may not fail; and once you have turned back, you must strengthen your brothers." There was a man who would fall from Christ after having attained to Him, and yet he was the one whom Our Lord would use as the heart and soul of all of the other Apostles.

Shakespeare despairingly cried, "The evil that men do lives after them; the good is oft interred with their bones." This is not always true in the Divine order. The greatest teaching about Divine grace and mercy comes from Augustine rather than Thomas Aquinas. Augustine was a man who once had evil in his heart, and then, like Peter, became the strength of his brethren. Our world is well-organized into groups, but what a change for the better there would be if men potent with the spell of Heaven went out like Peter to let their shadows fall upon evil lives and heal them.

*Freedom and Independence*

If St. Francis had been sent to a Siberian labor camp, or to a leper colony, or to a Wall Street brokerage firm, would he be any less a St. Francis? But how many mortals there are in the world who are one kind of character in need, another kind of character in plenty, who grumble amidst the uncomfortable, and who become possessed by possessions. St. Francis remains the same in all circumstances; the non-St. Francis types, like a chameleon, take on the color of the leaf on which they rest. Why the difference?

Because St. Francis is more free. That seems at first farfetched, but when is a man free? Negatively, he is free when he is not determined by outward circumstances, for example, when he is not in chains among prisoners, when he is not downcast with the despairing, when he is so far above environment as to be uninfluenced by it. He does not revolve around the world; the world revolves about him. It does not make his moods; he is free from moods. St. Paul said that he was content whether he abounded or whether he was in want.

But whence comes this psychological independence of the external, of maintaining an even spirit in a world of constantly changing lights and shadows? It comes from dependence on God. In fact, every true Declaration of Independence is a Declaration of Dependence. The Constitution of the United States makes its citizens independent of dictators, parliaments and even majorities as regards basic rights and liberties. But on what does it ground this independence? On the Declaration of Dependence, namely, "The Creator has endowed man with certain inalienable rights among which are the right to life, liberty and the pursuit of happiness." If our freedom came from the government, the government could take it away. It is only because our freedom has a theological foundation that it is "inalienable."

## Spiritual Inheritance

The United States has been an arsenal of defense against aggression; a Samaritan helping nations to rehabilitate themselves in peace; a pantry to the hungry and starving world; and, under Providence, the secondary cause for the preservation of the liberties of the free peoples of the world.

The moral and religious tone of our society has derived in part from our Declaration of Independence and our Constitution, which affirm: first, that rights and liberties are derived not from men or majorities, but from God and, therefore, are inalienable; second, because rights and liberties are God-given, citizens enjoy rights and liberties in addition to those given by the Constitution; third, the "people" and not the "masses" hold the title to civil power, which derives from God — the people being self-determined through conscience are opposite to the "masses," who are other-determined or dictator ruled.

Despite our rich national moral background, serious-minded citizens are concerned lest, like prodigal sons, we waste our spiritual inheritance through a decline in moral responsibility. Such a decay is due to two causes: first, forgetfulness that man must one day render an account of his steward-ship before the Eternal Judge; second, selfishness — a man cares most for those things to which he is bound organically, as he cares more for his head than his hat. As he becomes egotistic and separated from all organic bonds and social functions, such as Church, his country and his family, his sense of responsibility declines.

The consequences are many:

1. As persons surrender a sense of responsibil-ity to God, to the state, to family and to their vocation in life, they dissolve into atoms; atoms exist only for themselves. To say we live in the atomic age may be a more unfortunate characterization than we know; for if we are nothing but atomic individuals, then we are ready either to be split or

fissioned mentally, or else collectivized into a socialistic dictatorship. The latter is nothing but the forcible organization of the chaos created by a conflict of individual egotisms.

2. Once God and the moral law and conscience are exiled, then there is no standard outside of the crisis itself by which the crisis can be judged; no standard of time by which to set our watches, no score of music by which to distinguish our harmonies and discords.

3. Then science is left without a world of values, purposes, choices, ideals. The scientist himself, who is always a mind outside the facts he studies, is left without an *explanation* for all his descriptions. He is also without *truth* which he is always seeking in his experiments and which he knows exists and endures, even if the human race should go down to extinction.

4. Then *education* trains only half a man, developing his intellect, but not his will, his mind, but not his character; it gives him knowledge of facts, but gives him no purpose or destiny.

5. Finally, when Divine Truth is denied, there is no final determinant of truth except power, which has already enslaved one third of the world.

# ABIDING IN PEACE

## Cheerfulness

There are different ways of saying good-bye. When a Roman wished to say good-bye, he said, "Be well, be strong"; a Greek would say, "Be happy"; a Frenchman, a German and an Italian say, "Until I see you again." Actually what the word good-bye means is "God be with you." St. Paul always said good-bye through the word rejoice, or "be happy in the Lord." It was more than a wish; it was an exhortation. Our modern way of saying it would be, "Be cheerful in the Lord."

Cheerfulness is that quality which enables one to make others happy. It takes its origin half in personal goodness, and half in the belief of the personal goodness of others. It is the opposite of the morbid, the morose, the fretful, the grumbling, the somber.

But on the other hand, cheerfulness is not necessarily mirth. Mirth is short and transient, while cheerfulness is fixed and permanent. Mirth is like a flash of lightning; cheerfulness, like daylight. A merry person laughs, a cheerful person smiles. Mirth always requires the companionship of others to feed upon — social excitement, noise, jests, wisecracks, stories; but cheerfulness exists even when one is alone. That is why cheerful people very often sing to themselves.

The cheerful person always sees in any present evil some prospective good; in pain he sees a Cross from which will issue a Resurrection; in trial, he finds correction and discipline and an opportunity to grow in wisdom; in sorrow, he gathers patience and resignation to the Will of God. In all things, there is thankfulness.

Cheer may be natural, in which case it springs from an inborn vitality and zest of living. Even those who lack it can cultivate it to some extent, as marching music lessens fatigue. But there is another kind of cheerfulness which is Divine in origin. St. Paul bade others to have it as believing in God. This counsel he spoke to others in the midst of a storm at sea, promising them relief and rescue without loss of life. This kind of cheerfulness is found in Francis of Assisi, who expressed the joy of grace in his soul by song. St. Teresa of Avila, who lived a life of great penance, was wont to pour out her joy in that inner world of spirituality by clapping her hands and dancing in the Spanish style. In the history of the world there never has been a sad saint, because sanctity and sadness are opposites.

Helping others is not only the cause of cheerfulness, but also the fuel which keeps it burning. As Helen Keller, seeing through blindness, wrote, "Join the great company of those who make the barren places of life fruitful with kindness. The great enduring realities are love and service. Joy is the only fire that keeps our purpose warm and our intelligence aglow. Resolve to keep happy, and your joy shall form an invincible host against difficulty."

Paul and Silas sang in prison at midnight. And the only recorded time in the life of Our Blessed Lord that He ever sang was the night that He went out to His Death, which He called His Glory. I have met hundreds of missionaries who have survived death marches, who were tortured, brainwashed, starved and beaten, but I have never met one who said an evil word against those who did them wrong. They had no pleasure in what was done to them, but they had joy, for that was the gift of God.

Returning now to St. Paul's way of saying good-bye, namely, rejoice, he gives it a theological root. Having yielded the heart completely to Christ, he is at one with himself, and this harmony begets a joy that cannot be taken away.

A little girl who was not yet a Christian began to notice many pictures of Our Blessed Lord around the house when both her father and mother were converted. Her reflection was, "He always takes such a nice picture." Man of Sorrows though He was, "He rejoiced in spirit," and promised His followers that they would be partakers of His joy. We are made for His gladness and His cheerfulness, and we shall not be able to fulfill our destiny until we know how to be glad. Joy in the soul is nothing but the rising of the temperature on the thermometer of Divine Love.

## *Joy*

Joy is not the same as pleasure or happiness. A wicked and evil man may have pleasure, while any ordinary mortal is capable of being happy. Pleasure generally comes from things, and always through the senses; happiness comes from humans through fellowship. Joy comes from loving God and neighbor.

Pleasure is quick and violent, like a flash of lightning. Joy is steady and abiding, like a fixed star. Pleasure depends on external circumstances, such as money, food, travel, etc. Joy is independent of them, for it comes from a good conscience and love of God. At the Last Supper, Our Lord told His Apostles to keep His commandments, that "My joy may remain in you." This joy is related to nobility of character. Many enjoy themselves, but few have joy in themselves.

The saint can be joyful in pain and persecution, as Paul and Silas sang in prison amidst their torture, and as did the three youths in the fiery furnace. Pleasure can come from one organ of the body, such as the pleasure of eating; great joys are not produced by a single key, but where all instruments and keys vibrate together in their exuberant and inspiring symphony of virtue. Pleasure satiates and eventually turns to revulsion. Joy, however, never satiates. It is not a smile on the lips, but in the eyes and in the heart.

I once had dinner with twenty-two bishops who had come out from behind the Iron Curtain to attend the Second Vatican Council. All of them had suffered various kinds of persecution. One had been subject to brainwashing, followed by four years of torture in a prison; then he was put on a train which was deliberately wrecked, both his hips being broken. Another man had gasoline poured over him and was set afire; another told me he lived with his eighty-six-year-old mother on a few vegetables that he could grow in the garden and can for future use. Never once did any one of them speak of his persecution unless I asked; never was there any bitterness; I never found twenty-two more joyful men. They made one think of the words Paul applied to Our Lord: "Having joy set before Him, He endured the Cross."

Happiness is that which happens, like digging an oil well and getting rich. The word fortune is closely related to this kind of happiness, for it comes from being fortunate. Joy, however, is not the bliss of a condition, e.g., being rich or eating well, but of character. It is in the soul itself and literally implies a leap or a spring. The soul has such springs of life awakened within it that it exults from joy from within. In the ultimate analysis, only saints are joyful.

The joy born of love of God enables us to see the world from an entirely different point of view. Before, when shackled to the ego, we were cooped up within the narrow walls of space and time. But once the chains are broken, one falls heir to immensities beyond all telling. Then we find our greatest joys not in the things we cling to, but in what we surrender; not in the asking for anything, but the giving of something; not in what others can do for us, but in what we can do for others. Joy comes from using well the talents the Lord gave us, from a sense of bliss at being redeemed by Our Lord, and being permitted to minister more entirely to His Glory.

## *Angels*

Many people, having seen my "angel" clean my blackboard on television, will ask on meeting me, "How is your angel?" So, let us talk about angels and their role in our lives. But here we use the word angel in a very restricted sense — not as a spiritual invisible messenger, not a special illumination or a winged creature bearing a summons, not even as a vision or anything preternatural. By an angel we mean here any person or event that has changed the whole course of our life, influenced our behavior, made us turn right when we were about to turn left and in general made us better. What lifts such a concept out of the natural order is that sooner or later it is seen as being an act of God.

Take, for instance, the story of young Tobias, who was sent by his father Tobit to the land of Media on a kind of economic mission. His mother was worried about sending her son on such a long journey, so she went out and found a guide, whose name was Raphael. Raphael not only protected Tobias from dangers and helped him to collect a debt, but even found a good wife for him. The Book of Tobit says, "Raphael was an angel, but Tobias knew it not."

God sets many angels in our paths, but often we know them not; in fact, we may go through life never knowing that they were agents or messengers of God to lead us on to virtue, or to deter us from vice. But they symbolize that constant and benign intervention of God in the history of men, which stops us on the path to destruction or leads us to success or happiness and virtue.

God is generally operating behind secondary causes, like an anonymous benefactor. His direction of our lives is so hidden that most of us are unaware of how we were made an angel to help a neighbor, or how a neighbor was made an angel for us. When I finished college, I took an examination for a national scholarship worth several thousand dollars. I was anxious to complete my education by working to a Ph.D., but at the same time, ever since my earliest recollection, I had wanted to be a priest. Accepting the university scholarship would have meant postponing my call to the priesthood and maybe endangering it. During the summer vacation after college graduation, I visited our professor of philosophy and told him with great glee that I had won the university scholarship. He grabbed me by the shoulders and said, "Do you believe in God?" I told him the question was silly. But he challenged me, "But do you believe in God practically?" When I answered in the affirmative he said, "You know your duty. Go to the seminary now and begin studies for the priesthood. Tear up the scholarship."

But I protested, "Why cannot I work now for my Ph.D. and then go later to the seminary?"

He retorted, "If you make that sacrifice, I promise you that after your ordination to the priesthood you will receive a far better university education than before." I tore up the scholarship, followed my duty, and after ordination as a priest, I spent almost five years in graduate studies — most of them in some of the great universities of Europe. The professor was my angel. I saw it then, but I see it more clearly now.

Dr. Paul Tournier, who is one of the greatest of modern psychiatrists, says that for years his life was banal and confused, and never entrusted clearly to the guidance of God. Both he and his wife made such a commitment to Divine Guidance and found great happiness. As he put it in one of his books, "God led us step by step, from event to event. Only afterwards, as we look back over the way we have come and reconsider certain important moments in our lives in the light of what followed them, or when we survey the whole progress of our lives, do we experience the feeling of having been led without knowing it, the feeling that God has mysteriously guided us. We did not perhaps know it at the time. Time had to elapse to enable us to see it. But He opened the unexpected horizon to us."

Francis Thompson, speaking of the universality of this kind of angel, said, "Stir but a stone and start a wing." They are everywhere — good angels — only we do not recognize them as such. But the tragedy is that there are sometimes bad angels — they are evil persons who pull us down to vice. The world is a battlefield of angels.

## The Eyes of God

In pre-Christian times the word which the Greeks applied to God was *theos*. This word, it seems, was derived from the root *theisthai*, to see, because they regarded God as the all-seeing One. The eye which took in the whole universe at a glance was a knowledge beyond that of mortals. Still in the field of mythology, Momus, one of the heathen gods, was said to have complained of Vulcan that he had not set a covering in every man's breast, but rather that he had placed a glazed window on the darkest houses of clay to see what is done in them when no one else can see.

Linnaeus, the famous naturalist, was so much impressed by the fact of God's seeing and knowing all that he wrote over the door of his laboratory the Latin words, *"Innocui vivite; Numen adest"* — "Live innocently; God is here." Phidias, the great Greek sculptor, when he had completed the reclining statue of Theseus, was told that the statue was to occupy an elevated position in the temple. Observing that the back of the masterpiece was as highly polished as the front, he was asked why such a waste of time and energy when no one would see whether it was well finished or not. The sculptor reverently replied, "Men may not see it, but the gods will."

There is a legend about a Jewish Rabbi and the Emperor Trajan, who presented the difficulty that God should be everywhere and yet not be seen by mortal eyes. "I should like to see Him," said Trajan.

The Rabbi answered, "God's Presence is indeed everywhere, but He cannot be seen. No mortal eye can behold His glory."

The Emperor insisted. The Rabbi then suggested that they go and look at one of God's ambassadors. The Emperor assented. The Rabbi took him into the open air at noonday, and bade him look at the sun blazing in noonday splendor.

"I cannot see," said Trajan, "the light dazzles me."

The Rabbi answered, "You are unable to bear the light of one of these creatures; how then could you look upon the Creator? Would not such a light annihilate you?"

Hagar, the Egyptian maid, was fleeing with her son Ishmael from the wrath of Sarai. She called the name of the Lord Who spoke to her "the God of Vision." This eye of God is not to be thought of as an eye searching out our evil deeds. It is also a source of consolation, for it means that the Father's eye is filled with compassion, knowing all the trouble of our spirit, our hopes and our aspirations — even our failures.

What is it, however, in human nature which makes us feel that God always sees the bad things we do and rarely the good things? This makes God a kind of policeman, a moral certified accountant who writes only with red ink and never with black; not the God Who so loved man that He would send His Son as the Good Samaritan to take poor, weak, fallen human nature to the inn of refreshment and recovery. It is rather the evil which men do which makes them attribute this kind of detective eye to God. It is the deliberate wrong which makes us see God as Revengeful Justice.

From another point of view, God sees not the superficial self, but the real self; not the mask which we are wearing, but the heart behind it. The mask is that presentation we make to others in which we are careful to ignore or excuse all that is evil or faulty in us, and to magnify all that is good. How many would be willing to hide behind a hedge and hear their faults and failings described with accuracy by a neighbor? We would complain that it was not a real description of our mask. God's eye is fixed not on the phantom, but on him who creates it; not on the ideal, but on the actual.

The amazing thing is that God Who sees the series of our years gone by, as well as the marks that we have left upon our character, still loves us. This is really the truth of God's eye. He sees us with a Father's eye and loves us, wanderers though we may be, with a Father's heart.

## The Tenderness and Power

Pascal said there were two things that frightened him. One was his own heart; the other, the silence of the eternal spheres. Immanuel Kant, the German philosopher, held that the two things which awed him were the moral law within his breast and the starry firmament above. There has always been a tendency in literature to put these two together, and with a certain justice, for only a Power great enough to control the heavens could ever solace the individual heart.

The Hebrew psalmist was the forerunner of those who set in contrast the Providence of God, which was powerful enough to control the collective planets of the universe, and yet careful enough not to neglect the burden that weighed on a single heart. "He heals the brokenhearted, and binds up all their wounds. He tells the number of the stars; He gives them all their names."

There is hardly any physician or psychiatrist or friend who, in the face of a broken heart, would immediately think of countless stars or, contemplating the starry encampment of night, would ever think of the loneliness of the human breast. These are the two extremes which only great minds ever fit into one thought, namely, the bleeding heart and the fiery stars.

We lose the sense of the hour in studying history, and we forget the rolling scroll of history in the problem of an hour. It is the nature, however, of Divine Love to assure man that He Who takes care of the great universe is the only One to Whom man can trust his life. The sovereign balm for every wounded heart comes only from Him from Whose fingertips there tumbled planets and worlds. Many a man has felt his helplessness and loneliness beneath the stars, and yet Scripture says that star counting and heart healing go together.

There is a tendency today to believe that because the universe is far greater than we suspected, God perhaps is less perfect than we believed. This is part of the bad logic of Americans who judge the value of everything by its size. The truer point of view is that the greater the universe, the more certain man is to have his fretful mind lifted up to the thought of God's eternal Presence and Power. Then too, the fact that we unite the planets and the heart is proof that the sorrows of this life are not nearly as akin to earth as they are to heaven. The sadness of human hearts cannot be explained by any philosopher on this earth, but only by Him Who is powerful enough to make the stars and Who holds the secret of healing in His Own Divine Heart.

One finds the concretion and personalization of this relationship between hearts and stars in the contemplation of the Infinite God Who took upon Himself a human nature, and yet could be solicitous of one lost sheep, a woman taken in sin, a blind man, a thief and a brokenhearted widow following the body of her only son. It is not just sympathy that we need, but the consciousness that we are in the strong hands of the Lord of all. God is not remote from the little life down here on earth. We may ask how He could miss us from the fold when He is shepherding all the heavenly hosts. The answer is that God can find no room for His pity and no response to His love, nothing to bend over and heal and bless, except in our hearts. He Who holds all the nations in the palm of His hand is, nevertheless, the God of "Abraham and Isaac and Jacob." How often we say that it is very often the busiest person who is willing to help an individual. This is nothing but a confirmation that He Who made the heavens and lived for mankind spoke His tenderest Love when His audience was one listener. Everyone else is too weak to heal a broken heart. He alone can do it Who counts the stars.